CONTRA MARCUSE

ELISEO VIVAS

CONTRA

MARCUSE

ARLINGTON HOUSE   *New Rochelle, N.Y.*

Library of Congress Catalog Card Number 78-139890

ISBN 0-87000-112-4

MANUFACTURED IN THE UNITED STATES OF AMERICA

FOR WILFRID E. ZOGBAUM,

in the hope that he will live in
a world better than he was born into.

"Now I ask you: What can one expect from man since he is a creature endowed with such strange qualities? Shower upon him every earthly blessing, drown him in bliss so that nothing but bubbles would dance on the surface of his bliss, as on a sea; give him such economic prosperity that he would have nothing else to do but sleep, eat cakes and busy himself with ensuring the continuation of world history and even then man, out of sheer ingratitude, sheer libel, would play you some loathsome trick. He would even risk his cakes and would deliberately desire the most fatal rubbish, the most uneconomical absurdity, simply to introduce into all this positive rationality his fatal fantastic element. It is just his fantastic dreams, his vulgar folly, that he will desire to retain, simply in order to prove to himself (as though that were so necessary) that men still are men and not piano keys . . . even then he would not become reasonable, but would purposely do something perverse out of sheer ingratitude, simply to have his own way. And if he does not find any means he will devise destruction and chaos, will devise suffering of all sorts, and will thereby have his own way."

—Feodor Dostoevsky, *Notes from the Underground**

*From the book *Notes from the Underground* and *The Grand Inquisitor*, by Fyodor Dostoevsky. Translated by Ralph Matlow. Copyright © 1960, by E. P. Dutton & Co., Inc., Publishers and reprinted by their permission.

Contents

Preface

This is a polemical essay, directed at Marcuse's savage indictment of our society. It is not offered as an academic contribution. It has not been couched in the third person language that is loved by academics and does not pay attention to the rules laid down by our academic Emily Posts or even by the less restrictive academic Amy Vanderbilts. It often uses the first personal pronoun, and when it does not call a spade a spade, it refers to it as a manure shovel. It does not quite get down to the level of the academic New Left; it uses euphemisms like "manure" instead of the four-letter words that are frequently found in the writings of the new nihilists, both among academics and among students. I refrain from such language not because I am ignorant of four-letter words, but because that kind of language, having important functions to perform in extreme occasions, as I have explained elsewhere, ought not to be allowed to lose its value by everyday usage.

Marcuse has benefited a number of times from the way he has been treated by interviewers and critics who have ignored his savagery, overlooked his exaggerations, rancor, libelous criticism of our democratic and tolerant world. He has been written up as a sweet man endowed with the charm of an old-world courtesy, which no doubt he has; and his call for the destruction of our society, for direct action, for the shooting and murdering and repression of those who do not see the world with the hate-filled eyes he sees it with, has been soft-pedaled, it has not been exposed as the unreasonable criticism of our faults that it is. When I sat down to write this essay I had already made up my mind that I would not offer him the benefits others had offered him. He does not deserve our courtesy, our charity, our tolerance. He has proclaimed in writing the principle of intolerance towards those who disagree with him. There is no reason, unless one is a turn-the-other-cheek kind of Christian, to treat him differently from the way he treats his opponents. If he were to possess the power for a short while, he would out-Robespierre Robespierre, out-Saint-Just Saint-Just, and do better than Stalin and Hitler rolled into one. For this is an explicit, thought-out, and fundamental part of his ideology.

Marcuse is an advocate of what he sometimes calls "critical thinking," and at other times "the power of negative thinking." He uses this method to attack what he refers to as "the hell of our Affluent Society." His attack is radically partisan, thoroughly selective, utterly unsparing, merciless, without charity. A few times—one can count them on the fingers of one hand—he has a good word to say for Western society or for the United States. But for the most part, the radical critique of our world is systematically, methodically sustained, and coherent.

I have tried to turn Marcuse's method on his work. But while I use his method, there is a difference between his use of it and the use to which I have put it. My observations are critical but they are documented. What I have to say about his attack on our world is derived from his books and essays. I have not invented denunciations and libels that, having made them up, I proceed to attribute to him. I did not want to invent anything, but even had I wanted to I would have had no need, because Marcuse's attack is so extreme and so factitious that there is more than abundant evidence in his pages of his intellectual irresponsibility and of his poisoned animus.

In the book I have not done more than assert in general terms that some of his criticisms are without foundation, but I do not mean to suggest that our world is heaven on earth. We live in a better world, we fortunate ones, than man has probably ever lived in before. The majority of our citizens, and a large number of members of Western society outside the borders of the United States, enjoy opportunities that only a small minority ever enjoyed before. And we are earnestly seeking to expand the number of people who can enjoy these opportunities, in and out of the United States. But as an old ex-leftist— thank heaven I had the wits never to join any of the parties with which I cooperated in the Thirties—I know as well as

10

anyone who has lived in this country for as long as I have, and has kept his ears and eyes open, that the country is not perfect: its defects are many and serious. Its evils are real enough. How many of these can be traced, not to our social system or the American character, but to the human beings we are, no one knows today with certainty; but it is a safe guess that many of our faults are remediable. It is also, however, a fact that the whole nation, and the rest of the Western world, is directing its efforts to remedying those evils that can be done away with. But its virtues, let it be said with emphasis, do not make me an uncritical defender of it. I call myself a conservative, but I do not include in the meaning of the term what some of my friends on the Right include in it. I have no intention of glorifying the bourgeois world, or prettifying the faults of our industrial society or accepting uncritically its values. No man who thinks of himself as an autarch can do that. But above all, I have no use whatever for those men of the Right whom I think of as "dollar conservatives." These are men and women—I know a number of them—who would have no objection whatever to our society if they were exempted from paying taxes and could go back to the dog-eat-dog world of the robber barons.

Let us take a quick look at the defects of the American system. As the country expanded territorialy and grew in wealth and power, it was forced to improvise complex machinery to run the system. The ditch between its ideals and its reality is, in many respects, wide and deep, and perhaps growing wider and deeper. No man in his senses can deny this fact. But no man in his senses can deny the fact that the distance between the formulated ideals and the institutionalized actualities has been in many important respects reduced. The defects, however, cannot be denied. Our large cities cannot be governed. The problems they present are beyond the ingenuity and the good will of those who assume the responsibility of trying to govern them—granting that there is genuine good will, which I do solely on faith. That they could be governed by totalitarian methods I do not have any doubt. But that

11

the remedy would be worse than the disease I have no doubt either. Both organized and unorganized crime flourish and seem to be on the increase. Unorganized crime threatens the citizen physically. Organized crime is another invisible hand, of which Adam Smith probably had no knowledge, that contributes to the unhappiness and corruption of our citizens, sucks the wealth of the nation, and may ultimately lead to the destruction of our system of government. It would seem that unorganized crime could be dealt with successfully by the law. It is not. Organized crime is apparently beyond the reach of our law. It would seem that it can only be dealt with by means the use of which would be destructive of our democracy. It is as ruthless as ever a medieval baron was, but it displays an efficiency that no iron man on a horse could have displayed. All he could do was to stand at the pass and wait for a man who had business on the other side to come through. Our criminals are all over, and their power, we have long known, reaches over the men who govern the nation. It has been written that their sons now go to college and come out "educated" and ready to take over their fathers' nefarious business. The bureaucracy is to a large extent parasitical, but unavoidable. It grows with the growth in complexity of our technological society, and as it grows the freedom of the individual shrinks. The laws are today made by a bare majority of a small group of men sitting as supreme judges who have no regard whatever for the Constitution. What protects a man today is his anonymity. A prominent citizen can be hounded easily, if someone in power decides to take action. If a man in power was told by his father that steel men are SOB's, he can bring them to their knees. If a retired general agitates in favor of extreme opinions on the Right, those in power can move against him with the threat of committing him to a madhouse. Our Caesars have not yet gotten to the point where they can order a man to kill himself. But their discretionary power grows in alarming proportions.

American citizens, and to a lesser extent other members of Western society, enjoy a high standard of living. But those who live on a moderate fixed income, live in fear that destitution from inflation is around the corner. Health has improved and life is longer, and the progress of medical research is unquestionable. But medical expenses are a threat ever present to those who are no longer young, and better medicine means more people. The quality of life, the character of felt experience, is in many respects considerably better than it ever was for all except a small privileged minority in other nations at other times. More men enjoy today the *douceur de vivre* than Talleyrand could have imagined would ever be possible. A literate population—I did not say an educated one—can today enjoy life as it could not have been enjoyed in the past. The spiritual and the physical opportunities within the reach of any old Joe today would have been inconceivable a century or even fifty years ago, to anyone, however highly placed he might have been or whatever wealth or power he might have possessed.

But over this state of affairs hang a number of threats. Many of us are keenly aware of at least two of them and there seems to be little we can do to ward them off or drain their power. We seem to be nearly impotent before them. One is the threat of a world war, with its possible extermination of millions not only of our society but of other nations, if not of civilization itself. The other is the destruction of our society from within, by the wrecking work of intellectual termites who, be-doctored, balding, well-fed, and occupying influential positions in universities, the churches, newspapers, radio, and television, are gnawing at the uprights of our house. These people constitute, as we know, a small minority, but they are articulate, loud, and have a corner, so to put it, on the megaphones. Their goals are in sharp opposition to the ideals and values of the majority. In the last few years the academic sector of this minority has given convincing evidence that it has no respect whatever for the democratic process and that to a larger or smaller extent, they share Marcuse's hatred of the nation. Like Marcuse, they have nothing constructive to offer in place of that which they would destroy. All they do is gnaw away at values and virtues—in both the classical and the modern sense of the term—that made

13

this nation wealthy and powerful, and have enabled it to give its citizens the good life.

This minority despises discipline, courtesy; ignores decorum; holds patriotism in contempt, and relishes the spread of disintegration and divisiveness. The future threatens. Terror, fear, frustration go along with broader experience, with richer spirituality, and the larger and deeper possibility of self-fulfillment. We have grown used to the thought that we are probably living in the twilight of a civilization that does not have much time to go.

These are not the only defects of our world. Many others could be mentioned.

But having acknowledged the faults, how can I have a good word to say for our world? Am I not simply indulging in a flat contradiction? I am not, because with all its faults our world is, in many respects, nevertheless, a wonderful civilization, the best ever devised by man, progressively self-corrective, working still for knowledge, truth and human dignity, and the well-being, not of a minority, but of all its members, as they themselves conceive it. There is, therefore, no contradiction in pointing out defects while also pointing out high achievements. They do not cancel out. But to draw the balance it would take a man much wiser than any one of our new nihilists, much more irenic, much more humble before the facts, less dogmatic, much more capable of perceiving nuances, much more charitable, much more deeply acquainted with universal history and the history of the West since its early beginning among the Hebrews and Greeks.

But have no other critics of our society confirmed Marcuse's indictment? His fellow leftists, of course. But few of them have gone as far as he. Nor can we take them at their word. We must discount heavily what they say. There are, however, writers who cannot be called leftists, and much less New Leftists, who have made acute criticisms of our world. I have in mind two writers, Jaques Ellul and Friedrich George Juenger, men whose criticisms of our society are unsparing, well-documented, and

14

to a large extent unanswerable. Ellul formulates his criticisms as descriptions of our technological society and projections into the future of the goal towards which it is traveling, and it is frightening to envisage the goal. Juenger indicts. But both are objective and do not accuse out of the obvious hatred that animates Marcuse against our world. If Marcuse were as objective as either Ellul or Juenger, if he expressed himself without rancor, if he did not exaggerate, above all if he could be specific about the domination we are supposed to be the victims of, his writing would carry a much heavier burden of truth than it does. But of course it would not become the bible of the new nihilists.

If our world has faults, as I have just admitted, how can we object to Marcuse's critique? The objections emerge from a number of features of his attack, some of which I will point out in the text. But it is not superfluous to summarize the important ones here. The first is that the serious faults I have just pointed out do not engage Marcuse. He rants against automobiles and split-level homes, but does not dwell on the air-pollution the automobile creates. He accuses the United States of being an aggressive nation, and bewails the fact that the attempted coup of the Indonesian communists did not succeed (can you imagine how they would have dealt with their enemies?), but is indifferent to, or unaware of, the effects of advancing technology on the freedom of men. The threat to freedom is not the result of human domination, as he holds, but of the enslavement of man by techniques, in the specific way in which Jaques Ellul analyzes the process. What concerns Marcuse is the conviction that we are the victims of deliberate domination; and worse, that we are happy in our condition. This domination of which we are allegedly the victims is stated by him in generalized terms, and is measured against a vague notion of freedom that never comes to terms with the actualities of social living. The chief defect of his criticism is that it is made *in vacuo,* in accordance with criteria that are abstract, futuristic, devoid of any historical perspective. Had he been less speculative and more concrete he would have had to make comparisons that would have forced him in turn to qualify his libels.

To be admissible a criticism of our society has to be made in the proper historical perspective and has to be comparative. It should measure our defective present by comparison with our defective past and its possibly less defective—not perfect—future. But this is not the way Marcuse measures our present. He does not note any progress in humaneness, he does not admit that the quality of the life we live is better than it was for our ancestors. He is an absolutist, measuring our society not by what it has been, is, and is trying to be, but by an abstraction. This formula, he claims, is drawn from "reason"—as if reason were an organ capable of delivering substantive propositions, like the alleged ideal of freedom from the tyranny of the genital. These alleged ideals or goals are not derived from reason, either Marcuse's or anyone else's. They are probably drawn from his own frustrations: "probably," for it would take a complete psychoanalytic dossier to locate their source in his experience. Wherever they arise from, his criticisms are evidence of a total failure to reckon with our plight and the efforts being made to improve our world. He is blind, stone-blind, to the qualifications that he would have to offer for his indictment to be taken seriously. The alternative he proposes, in all seriousness, involves two parts. For the individual, a vague hedonism that would take us back to the pre-genital stage of development, *not* to any of the previous stages marked off by Freud, but to a polymorphous eroticism. For society, an equally vague socialism in which domination would be done away with, and men would be free to play and display as they saw fit.

My objection to his criticism does not arise merely from its false accusations, his factitious indictments, the utter irresponsibility of his goals. It also arises from the temper that is expressed in his pages. It is arrogant, it is apodictic, it admits of no questioning, it is despotic, it is overweening, it is the expression of utter certitude that it is in complete possession of the truth, in possession of a conviction that what is stated can only be disagreed with by vicious men. The inhumanity shown to the poor forked radish in his plight—in plainer terms, the contempt expressed for individuals and the idealization of the abstraction *man*—is unrestrained. Marcuse does not try to hide

16

from the reader the depth of his bigotry, the self-righteous spirit of a man who, were he able to use the word "God," could say with Saint-Just: "God, protector of innocence and virtue, since you have led me among evil men it is surely to unmask them!" When one looks at his violent followers from a perspective other than that which reveals them as wreckers, one sees that they are sheep. For what other creature could accept such bigotry, such overweening, prideful despotism, and take its ukases as if they were liberating words?

Marcuse accuses our society of being sick. It is. It suffers from various diseases. So have been, so are, and so will be, probably, all human societies until the end of time. But the most serious malady from which ours suffers is that it has fostered the appearance in its midst of men of erudition and intelligence who are monsters of impiety and are using all their powers to destroy the sources of their being.

It is my duty, but a most enjoyable one, to express my deep-felt thanks to those who helped me to accomplish this job. First, of course, my wife, whose secretarial labors considerably eased the task and whose faith and encouragement and critical acuity, helped me throughout; to Robert H. Baker, Dean of the Graduate School of Northwestern University, who was influential in securing a grant for the typing of the manuscript, and to the Research Fund that made the grant; and to the Relm Foundation, whose generous aid enabled me to give my time to the reading and writing that went into the making of this book.

Rockford College,   ELISEO VIVAS
Rockford, Illinois
13 April 1970

For bibliographies of Marcuse's works see *The Critical Spirit, Essays in Honor of Herbert Marcuse,* ed. by Kurt H. Wolff and Barrington Moore, Jr., Boston, 1967, and Robert W. Marks, *The Meaning of Marcuse,* New York, 1970.

Thanks are due to Beacon Press for permission to quote from Marcuse's books. Works cited in the text have been abbreviated as follows:

R & R   *Reason and Revolution. Hegel and the Rise of Social Theory.* 2nd edition with a supplementary chapter. New York, 1963.

E & C   *Eros and Civilization. A Philosophical Inquiry into Freud.* Boston, 1955.

S M   *Soviet Marxism. A Critical Analysis.* New York, 1969.

O-D M   *One-Dimensional Man. Studies in the Ideology of Advanced Industrial Society.* Boston, 1966.

C P T   *A Critique of Pure Tolerance.* Boston, 1965. This book contains three essays; the last one, entitled "Repressive Tolerance," is by Marcuse.

E L   *An Essay on Liberation.* Boston, 1969.

E & S   *Ethics and Society.* Edited by Richard T. De George. Garden City, N. Y., 1966. "Ethics and Revolution" is by Marcuse.

M & MM   *Marx and The Modern World.* Edited by Nicholas Lobkowicz. Notre Dame, London, 1967. "The Obsolescence of Marxism" is by Marcuse.

The following books have been cited:

MacIntyre, Alasdair,   *Marcuse,* London, 1970.

Marks, Robert W.,   *The Meaning of Marcuse,* New York, 1970.

Robinson, Paul A.,   *The Freudian Left,* New York, Evanston and London, 1969.

The following essays have also been cited:

Cranston, Maurice,   "Herbert Marcuse," *Encounter,* Vol. XXXII. No. 3, March, 1969.

Kaleb, George,   "The Political Thought of Herbert Marcuse," *Commentary,* January, 1970.

CONTRA MARCUSE

A SPECTRE HAUNTS OUR WORLD—THE SPECTRE OF NIHIL-
ism. The spectre Marx and Engels let loose on their world was
a calamitous threat. But it had a saving grace. They had in mind
the destruction of our society in order to create, as they
claimed, a world without iniquity and exploitation. The spectre
that haunts our world proposes nothing but destruction.

Contemporary nihilism has no plans to build a better world
and it boasts that it has not. It is bent on destruction for the sake
of destruction. Will it be able to bury the corpses it will create?
Will it be able to clear the rubble that will follow the demoli-
tions it will stage? This is doubtful, since all it wants is to
destroy, to wreck. It condemns as evil all that now ministers to
our life. The "philosopher" *en titre* of this movement makes
two exceptions. But we shall see that no exception can be

made. All else is condemned as evil: the whole of our society is worthless, all that we take pride in no less than what we too recognize as evil and try to correct. It judges all there is as fit only for the flaming bottle, and later the wrecking ball and the stick of dynamite. Will it use the healing bulldozer? Not likely.

I put the word philosopher in quotes, above, because to call Marcuse's thought philosophy, without indicating an incongruity, is to dishonor a noble word. Dante called philosophy *un amoroso uso di sapienza*—a loving use of wisdom. This is a definition that unfolds slightly the etymological meaning of the word, by making explicit its practical function. Marcuse has no wisdom to put to use. Knowledge he has, diluted in gallons of extremist opinion. And he uses the mixture not to sweeten the world lovingly, but to destroy it in hatred. One does not have to read him extensively to learn that from his pages arises an asphyxiating vapor, corrosive in its animosity. He voices a total rejection of the society that gave him refuge, that has put him in the upper-income bracket for academics, and that has piled on him honors that no man openly advocating it should have given him: academic posts, research appointments, two professorships in two universities of distinction, and at least one offer (that he did not accept) from another, which I happen to have learned of; government employment, invitations to lecture at distinguished academic institutions, an honorary degree, a book of essays in his honor to which a number of scholars who no doubt think of themselves as responsible contributed; and apparently an all-out effort by the Department of Philosophy and the administration at San Diego to retain him on its staff. He was elected President of the Pacific Division of the American Philosophical Association for 1968-69. The larger part of the honors come from full-fledged academics and some have been conferred on him at a time when rioting students, proclaiming him one of their sources of inspiration, were threatening to destroy the universities of the nation. The state protects his "right" to utter outrageous slanders against it while he accepts its benefits. It protects his life when some kooks threaten it—as in our society it is its duty. Where in the world of the Left, which he prefers to our democratic world, would he get away with the kind of activity he carries on?

It would be injurious to us, however, if we failed to recognize that not all the faults of which he accuses us were made up out of whole cloth. Some of them are real faults. Where there are men organized bureaucratically, there is misuse of power, and we have it among us. But all our faults, those he invents and those he discovers and exaggerates, are expressed in a tone that proclaims the infallibility of the writer.

There are many intellectuals in agreement with this totally negative attitude of pure hatred, educated men anticipating in ecstasy the vertigo of total destruction. The majority of these nihilists do not belong to the most deprived class of our society. The group is made up of university professors and the students whom they pervert to their destructive vision, teachers of the grade schools, members of the clergy, and professional men in law and even medicine and engineering, the last two, professions that have traditionally recruited conservative people.

The workers and the majority of the inhabitants of the technologically advanced countries of the West know they are sharing the benefits of prosperity. They do not want to destroy our world; what they want is a bigger share of its affluence than they now take home. They know they have nothing to gain by wrecking the political and industrial system that makes possible the good life they live. They want two cars, whereas at present in the United States the majority owns only one. They want television sets and, of late, colored television, a longer paid vacation, home appliances to make life easier for their wives, schooling for their children; they want gadgets. In my teaching years I have had in my classes, training for white-collar professions, the sons and daughters of laborers: young people who looked forward to a better, or at least more prestigious life than their parents had lived. Their hope was made possible by their parents and by our society. Some of them are now respected professors, lawyers, and a few of them doctors, in spite of the frightful cost of medical training. In short, what they want, and what is today much easier to get than it was over forty years ago when I began teaching, is what in our

23

Western World is taken to be the good life. And many of them manage to live it. The average member of our society would be happier if there were less crime and if we were not at war with the communists who work to destroy us. But when the red and the black are added up and compared, he knows that as far as living is concerned he's in the black.

But he does not dream of freedom *in vacuo*. That's for the Marxist intelligentsia and the new nihilists who know they will be well equipped with Lubiankas and concentration pens to throw us into, should they ever—God forbid—"liberate" us from our repressors. The American worker leaves abstract slogans and theoretical political formulas to the members of the intellectual Cosa Nostra: the New Left, with its fabricated causes, its histrionic grievances, and its abstract humanitarianism. What right then have profoundly alienated men, men who have no ties to a communal body, to tell us that what we want is false? They are outsiders who know nothing about us; they can only speak to their own kind, pure nihilists, the wreckers whose chief problem, today, is that they have been deprived of something to complain about.

But it begins to look as if these men will continue the nefarious work until all of us, including of course no small number of them, will rot in the ruins of a world they intend to bring down on our heads. For when the walls and roofs begin to fall many of them will no more be able to run to safety than we shall.

These men speak of our "sick society." The charge, as used, is no more than mere propaganda. But Herbert Marcuse has tried to examine the meaning of the expression and give it a rationale. And this points to the role he plays in the nihilist movement. He is the thinker who has expressed for the nihilists their unshaped anger, their subjective rejections, their frustrations, real and imaginary; who rationalizes their nihilism in quasi-philosophical formulas based on specious factual charges and on an *a prioristic* notion of human perfection that has very little to do with human reality. When we understand what Marcuse has in mind as a substitute for the imperfect world in which we live, this ideal seems to us contemptible, repugnant and odious. We do not find it difficult to see that, were we to

24

accept it, it would lead us to vacuity, meaninglessness and consequent despair.

Appealing to the worst of the worst among us, in the last few years Marcuse has emerged as the philosopher *en titre* of the new nihilists. It is important to place emphasis on the adjective "new," because the old nihilists of Russia—bomb throwers, assassins, men and women in determined opposition to the existing state—had a vision of a new society; not well delineated, and incompatible with human reality it was, nevertheless, a positive dream. But as already indicated, and as is generally recognized, the new wreckers and their "philosopher" have no positive program. Indeed, one of Marcuse's boasts is that no positive program is possible under the repressive system in which we live. This assertion is not consistent with his doctrine of the essence of man, and it is a recent development of his thought. But when, as in *Eros and Civilization,* he suggested an alternative to our condition all he could offer us was a vague notion of resexualized man, working little and laboring, if possible, not at all; man, as he puts it, "playing and displaying." It is thus obviously imperative that we examine his doctrine.

BUT THE CRITIC OF HERBERT MARCUSE DOES NOT FACE AN easy task. True, if he adopts Marcuse's own doctrine of complete intolerance against views he disagrees with, and if he uses Marcuse's own methods, a critic can, *a machetazos,* without much effort, chop up Marcuse's views into kindling. But this approach will not do for a serious scholar trying to understand and evaluate, with an honest purpose, Marcuse's total condemnation of our world. The critic must seek to judge honestly the articles of Marcuse's indictment. To attain and keep the required attitude he must jump over a number of obstacles that Marcuse puts in his way, and these are formidable. Whether I shall be able to jump over these obstacles or not I cannot tell, until my effort is submitted for criticism to honest and fair-minded critics. But neither Marcuse nor any of his followers can claim the right to criticize those they oppose. For Marcuse has denied them the right to expect from him and his followers any kind of tolerance whatever.

It would seem as if Marcuse writes to elicit anger on the part of those who disagree with him. If he does, this is an objective he accomplishes with ease. One has to shrug one's shoulders at his exaggerations of the defects of our society, including idiosyncratic resentments that are altogether trivial.

There is also his manner of argument; or, more precisely, his technique of asseveration and apodictic assertion. Alasdair MacIntyre writes of it in the following manner: Marcuse's whole manner of thought and style of presentation "does not invite questioning, but suggests that the teacher is delivering truths to the pupil which the pupil has merely to receive." (*Marcuse*, London, 1970, p. 17) And he goes on to tell us that Marcuse does not give us any reason to believe that what he writes is true. He illustrates his points but never offers evidence in a systematic way. But above all, MacIntyre finds Marcuse never considers the difficulties that arise for his position. Is this not to say that Marcuse is not a philosopher but a prophet who takes himself to be fully authorized to lay down the doctrine? Another writer, Robert W. Marks, in an ambivalent study, *The Meaning of Marcuse* (New York, 1970, p. 79), writes:

> Marcuse is a master of the polemics of obscurity. His meanings are seldom completely clear even to the reader who approaches him with the necessary background and with sympathetic interest.

Further on (p. 97), Marks tells us, "The essential conclusion, perhaps, is that Marcuse is not so much a philosopher of revolution as a pamphleteer. He is an exhorter—in the tradition of the Nietzsche of *Zarathustra.*"

There is, finally, the serious problem of understanding what he writes, to be discussed below.

These aspects of his work make up an almost impregnable abatis. When the reader tries to get past it to the core of intelligible thought behind it he finds his energy draining, his capacity to concentrate disappearing, and in their place he finds himself filled with a subtle irritation. The attitude elicited by these obstacles and the weakening effort to overcome them draws him, before he is clearly aware of it, into a mood of opposition to what he is reading, which can easily heat up into as irascible a rejection of Marcuse's thought as one of Marcuse's own irrational "negations."

An examination of Marcuse's thought is not complete when one has finished looking into his judgments and assessed their validity. A rancid air of subjectivity hangs about almost everything he has to say, and one cannot avoid the question: "I wonder what makes him say that, since it is so far from what one knows of our world?" Something has bruised him deeply. Hatred so intense, so implacable, so pure, must have a root deep in the soul. What has caused it? Could it have been generated by the trauma of his exile? I do not think so. But the students who eat out of his hand give you an account of an extremely sweet man, courteous, with an endearing old-world courtesy, a man who is really concerned with their growth. It would be of immense value to know what in our world and in his own experience caused the misery of rejection in which he seems to live. Are there not some things in our age, in our world, that he finds good? Some piece of music or poetry, friends, man or woman, or a good meal with good wine; a clear, cool morning in the country, or an evening by the sea? In a recently published interview the writer tells us that Marcuse loves good music and good food. But from his books the reader does not get the least inkling that Marcuse ever found life worth living. If his books, particularly *One-Dimensional Man,* are evidence, Marcuse has not lived an hour for which he can feel piety and which he would care to live again.

Although a psychological problem the solution of which neither validates nor invalidates his indictment of our society, this problem is not irrelevant to those seeking light on attitudes that are by no means rare among us. I am convinced that the new nihilists constitute a smaller minority than their publicity agents claim it to be. But it must be acknowledged that recently they have pre-empted the center ring and they have put

28

on performances that have enormous theatrical value. But whether there are a large number of these people around or whether they are only a small but loud minority, an understanding of their subjective motivations would be an important contribution to the objective knowledge of their repudiation of our world.

Unfortunately the information I have about Marcuse is only that which has appeared in newspapers and magazines. Before Marcuse gained a worldwide reputation as one of the intellectual leaders of the new nihilists, he had achieved academic success in the United States. But even since he became the recognized "philosopher" of nihilism, after he moved to California, he has continued to receive academic recognition. I have been told by a colleague of his at Brandeis that his student followers accepted him uncritically as a prophet, a Führer of a political-intellectual ideology which his followers neither questioned nor allowed anyone to question. The man who gave me this information was speaking of Marcuse's followers at the time that they were reading *Eros and Civilization;* my own encounters with Marcuseans indicate that they are imbued with the nihilistic ideas of *One-Dimensional Man.* But I feel confident that they will take to his next publication with the same ardor with which they took to previous ones, although as I shall say again, there is not much digestible food in *Negations* for those of his followers who are not trained in philosophy— preferably German philosophy up to the time Hitler came to power.

What in our world turns gifted and fortunate men like Marcuse into irreconcilable nihilists? Their bill of particulars does not account for their feelings. Were Marcuse only one of a few nihilists, we would be justified in assuming that an exhaustive explanation could be found in their psychiatric dossiers. But given the fact that a bitter nihilism seems to have spread over large areas of the globe, its source cannot be merely psychological. We are faced with a baffling social problem. Fortunately it is not one to which we need turn here.

The problem is all the more baffling since at no earlier time in the history of our world, so far as we can tell, did so many men enjoy the material and spiritual benefits and opportunities we take for granted in our society today. There are, of course, enough iniquities and cruelties in our society to keep the reformers, radicals, activists and bleeding-hearts, busy till Kingdom-come. But no allowance is made by the nihilists for the saving grace, no account taken of the genuine improvements, no credit given by Marcuse, at least in the last years of his work, for those efforts and solid accomplishments that could, that should, lead to a softening of his vitriolic repudiation of our world.

True, there is hunger in the world still, and in some parts of the globe life is cheap. But to give an account of evil and not to notice, in passing, at least, what is being done to improve the conditions in which men live is merely to contribute to the evil that is being objected to.

LET US TURN TO MARCUSE'S WORK. I CANNOT EVALUATE THE soundness of the scholarship of his first book to appear in the United States. *Reason and Revolution* (Preface dated, 1941), since its subject, as its subtitle indicates, *Hegel and the Rise of Social Theory,* is not within my competence. But to the fact that the book displays broad erudition in its field and to the fact that Marcuse attacks his problem in a thoroughly scholarly manner, anyone who has skimmed a chapter or two can testify with confidence. Stalinists did not like Marcuse's version of Marx. A former Stalinist, Frank Meyer, told me recently that he had written a withering criticism of the book for a Party magazine when the book first appeared. But allowing for the disagreements that flourish normally among exegetes in philosophy and the social sciences, and allowing for partisan intransigence, I doubt whether one could justly reject the scholarship of the book. Marcuse's *Soviet Marxism,* a later book, is a condemnation of Communist Russia. But it is nevertheless a scholarly examination of developments in Russia after the October Revolution, and it is thus mild in comparison with the virulent attacks on our society to be found in *One-Dimensional Man.*

I cannot praise *Eros and Civilization* in the same manner. The book is a sustained effort to invalidate the thesis of Freud's *Civilization and Its Discontents* and the effort, in my opinion, fails dismally. Marcuse matches the facts of our actual social system against a hedonistic dream which he tries to pass off as a "rational" system in which men will put very little time into "working"—for "labor" shall be abolished—and the rest of the time in "play and display"—about which nothing is said in specific terms. We are up against faith and hope and against neither of the two can there be argument.

To me, the reason for Marcuse's failure to avoid Freud's conclusion about the price we must pay for civilization or culture, is that Marcuse does not grasp the depth of Freud's radical predicament. Freud's thesis, as is well known, is that what in the English translation is called "civilization" refers to the institutions created by the sublimated expression of our repressed "instincts." (Note in passing that the term "civilization" is used by Freud in both an honorific sense and also to refer to what American sociologists would call "culture.") Freud argues that sublimation can never achieve complete satisfaction of our repressed instincts, and this is the source of our ineradicable discontent. No human creation—no religion, art, morality, science, or play—can possibly satisfy that "chaos," that "cauldron of seething excitement" that is the Id.

Marcuse argues that we can avoid Freud's gloomy conclusion if we distinguish between "labor" and "work." Labor is the result of domination (a very important term in Marcuse's thought), enforcing "surplus repression" and bringing about alienation and misery. "Surplus repression" is the repression of workers and, in our society, of everybody, required to maintain exploitation for the benefit of the few interested in keeping the system afloat. It is surplus, it is unnecessary, because a "rational" system, a socialism never more than vaguely sketched, would release man from the fetters he now carries and would enable him to play and display with considerably less "labor" than he now has to put into keeping alive or keeping the system afloat. But it is better to let Marcuse express his utopian dream in his own words:

> Man is free only when he is free from constraint, external and internal, physical and moral—when he is constrained neither by law nor by need. But such constraint *is* the reality: Freedom is thus, in a strict sense, freedom from the established reality: man is free when "the reality loses its seriousness" and when its necessity "becomes light" *(leicht)*. "The greatest stupidity and the greatest intelligence have a certain affinity with each other, in that they both seek only the *real*"; however, such need for and attachment to the real are "merely the results of want." In contrast, "indifference to reality" and interest in "show" (display, *Schein*) are tokens of freedom from want and "a true enlargement of humanity." In a genuinely humane civilization, the human existence will be play rather than toil, and man will live in display rather than need. (*E & C*, p. 187. Italics in text)

This is to Marxify Freud. But it is inadmissible for reasons I am going to take up in some detail below.

To assume that man can be free from constraint by law is to assume the possibility of institutionalizing some sort of pure anarchistic society. This is an impossible feat, since an anarchic institution is a contradiction in terms. But let that go. It is obvious that in the overpopulated world in which we live nothing but a complex industrial system could fend off a major world catastrophe. That men could be free from some of the needs they now have—only some—seems thinkable, given our technological resources. But much more needs be known about our needs before the problem could be meaningfully discussed.

When Marcuse writes of the gratuitous cruelty of our present misery and of the felicity that the transference of the libido will bring about, he writes like a religious man longing for a second birth and full redemption. In spite of the jargon, the tone of his expression reminds one of the anguish and hatred of this world and the longing for another one that we find in gnostic texts about the time of Christ of which Hans Jonas wrote. For the religious man it is sin that crushes the soul; for Marcuse it is mundane frustration. But in intensity of anguish and longing they are at one. We do not find in Marcuse's pages the controlled eloquence with which Norman O. Brown writes about the resurrection of the body and what man will be like when he becomes "polymorphically perverse." There are passages in Brown's *Life Against Death* that have the genuinely poetic quality of the best religious prose.

Marcuse never manages to reach such heights, but there are a few passages in which his words almost manage to leave the ground. Like a hen trying to fly, he flaps his verbal wings and jumps in a jerky way, and you understand what he is trying to do: he is trying to express in what for him are lyric terms, the fervor of his yearning. At such times one may not have sympathy for the object of his longing, for his radical hedonism, but one cannot help brooding in pity about the intense frustration from which such longing must have arisen. The hatred of all that is, the longing for a blessed life beyond this present harsh world, is not a rare experience for human beings. Is there one among us who is so unimaginative or invulnerable, so unwounded, that he has not entertained visions of a better life? Whether the goal is projected beyond this world, or read forward or backwards in history, probably the same affective soil feeds the longing.

IT WOULD TAKE A LONG ESSAY TO EXAMINE WITH ADEQUATE
thoroughness Marcuse's effort to disprove Freud's thesis, and
another even longer effort to explore his notion of the supreme
good and show that it would turn us, not as he believes, into
free men, but into strange creatures, old babies engaged, as a
student recently put it to me, in an all-day thumb-sucking state
of euphoria. Let me assert with emphasis that the energy involved in the examination would be fully justified, just as the
energy put into an examination of Norman O. Brown's *Life
Against Death* is fully justified.

Let us stop briefly to ask what Marcuse means by "playing
and displaying," for this phrase expresses an important component of his vision of a better world. He holds that a more
equitable distribution of the goods we are able to produce

today because of our technological advances would reduce the "labor" that a repressive society still demands of its members, and would increase the capacity for work and play. "Labor" would be done away with, "work" would be increasingly reduced, although some work will always remain necessary, but certainly not as much as is exacted from us today. The rest of the time would be put into "the free play of human faculties and desires." (*E & C,* p. 295) Along with this transformation would go the transformation of sexuality into eros. Human beings would no longer be under the tyranny of the genital. No longer used exclusively as machines for the performance of exacted labor, they would be "resexualized," that is, human beings would undergo a reactivation of all erotogenic zones: genital supremacy would decline and pregenital polymorphous sexuality and narcissism would take its place. In the following pages I shall write about either "resexualizing" or "reëroticizing" the individual. This will take place when we return him to a condition prior to the development of the genital phase, of which Freud speaks. The resexualized body will "regress"—but not at all in the pejorative sense, but rather in an eulogistic one—to polymorphic and narcissistic sexuality through a "reactivation of all erotogenic zones"; it will undergo the eroticization of the entire personality, which is to say that non-libidinal relations in which he is involved at present under repression will become eroticized. Let me put it briefly this way: with the decrease of repression and labor Eros will take dominion over all of life, and we will live a life of play and display. Put in still different words, there will be no need to make passes at girls with or without glasses. You will drift towards her and she towards you and you will fondle each other sweetly your whole reëroticized bodies, but there will be no thought of a trip to a motel.

That some men suffer from the tyranny of the genital, on which Marcuse dwells with resentment, is no figment of his imagination. Consider the evidence: we have knowledge of religious sects and of early Christian "saints" who willingly emasculated themselves. The followers of Cybele did it, although it did not prevent them from indulging in sexual orgies during the celebrations to their goddess. A Russian sect practiced it, the Skoptsy, at least until the October Revolution. However, that the resentment against the tyranny of the genital is universal, is simply not credible, and to assert it responsibly would call for evidence that Marcuse—whose habit of making facts by executive fiat operates here—does not seem to feel the need of supplying. Consider that a proto-Kinsey survey I remember published in the middle Twenties reported the variations of sexual needs among people to be quite wide, and Kinsey did not claim that all men were capable of the feats of his famous lawyer. Were the facts to be gathered with care, they would enable us to take the first steps in finding out exactly to what extent men and women do suffer from the tyranny of the genital. Until we have solid and broad knowledge about the sexual drives among humans and the factors that control them, we cannot speak responsibly about them. Knowledge, pursued with care, would finally take us quite far afield. For instance, it would tell us how many men and women who do not suffer from the tyranny of the genital are frigid and how many are "normal." Turned from a purely speculative to a factual problem, the notion becomes fruitful and perhaps capable of illuminating many dark regions of human nature. Made the subject of pure speculation, it is an instance—the reader of this study will find many such—of what we could call Marcuse's empirical irresponsibility.

But what exactly is the "display" which, added to play, would make up the substance of human life? Apparently men, free from want, would be indifferent to the present established reality, which for them would lose its "seriousness," since it would no longer have any power over them. The indifference to the reality of want would introduce an interest in "show"—which, as we saw, between parentheses is said to be "dis-play," *Schein.* When present, show or display would constitute a true "enlargement of humanity."

With the term "play" we should have no trouble, but I know I have not yet given the reader an adequate grasp of the basic term "display." Let me try to elucidate the notion. The reality that loses seriousness is the reality of want and need, the present reality, in which we are forced to live under domination, under repression. Reality loses its seriousness when our wants and needs can be satisfied, as Marcuse puts it, without alienated labor. A contrast between the business man and the stereotypical picture of the artist might throw some light on the meaning of the term. But it should be borne in mind that the contrast does not really hold for Marcuse, because the artist in our society is, in a strict sense, no more free than the entrepreneur. But let us assume that he is free, while we squares are not. He is, because he disdains our norms, he disregards our moral codes and proprieties; he has no concern for the world that we are concerned with and "take seriously."

We walk up the dilapidated stairs and dark hall into the artist's studio, and find him working intensely with some bits of colored paper, a pot of glue, and some wire. We ask him what he is up to, and he shrugs his shoulders. "Just trying to see what will come out." "What does it mean?" we ask. There is an ill-suppressed tone of irritation in his answer: "Nothing, just trying." An artist has any number of ways of distinguishing a right guy from a square, and one of them is that the latter is always asking what something the artist happens to be playing with *means.* If we are not altogether ninety-degree squares we keep quiet and watch. Our artist is playing with geometric forms and displaying his skill; the paper, wire, and glue are *displaying* their potentialities. Marcuse ends the discussion of "play" and "display" as follows:

> Then man is free to "play" with his faculties and potentialities and with those of nature, and only by "playing" with them is he free. His world is then display *(Schein),* and its order is that of beauty. (*E & C,* p. 188)

The result envisaged is a total transformation of the lives we live—or, more exactly, of the animals we are. Nature would not dominate man, as it does in primitive society, nor would it be dominated by man, as in the civilization in which we live, "the established civilization." Nature would then be an object of contemplation. Released from violent domination and exploi-

38

tation, nature would become free "to display the wealth of its purposeless forms . . ." And he concludes the paragraph as follows: "Beyond want and anxiety, human activity becomes *display*—the free manifestation of potentialities." (*E & C*, p. 190)

If the meanings of these two basic terms still remain vague —as I believe they do—let me try to add a bit to their elucidation by saying that man would live in the enjoyment of his body, he would live for the sake of pure enjoyment and not for the sake of producing goods or performing activities for which there would be no longer any need. In the context of his discussion, where the emphasis falls on bringing back to sensitivity erotogenic zones that have lost their capacity for response, it is obvious, in spite of an assertion to the contrary to be discussed below, that the mind would have no important role to play in the activities of resexualized man. But it is difficult to believe that an intellectual would be happy unless he could use his mind to the full. But how a person bent on polymorphic pleasure-seeking would also engage in mental activity is difficult to see. What Marcuse seems to have in mind is the kind of unburdened primitive life that some Europeans and Americans of the Nineteenth Century believed men could live in the South Sea Islands when the whites began to discover them. But we cannot be certain because he writes in vague, abstract terms. All we can be certain of is that Marcuse's conception of the good society is filtered through the red lenses of Marx and is conceived in partial opposition to Freud. Since he does not have the slightest trace of the novelist in him, he can only assert in Marcusean language the faith and hope that animate him.

Kindly note with some care that it is only on the basis of hope and faith that Marcuse is ready to destroy our world. What other ground could he have for his belief in the realization in the future of a contingent historical event? We know his answer; he has "Reason," whose omnipotence is capable of delivering any thing he wants. In an essay entitled "Ethics and Revolution" that appeared in a collection of essays by various hands, titled *Ethics and Society* (1966), we are assured in passing that a revolution can be justified as ethically, and not merely politically, right if "rational grounds" can be presented "for its chances to grasp real possibilities of human freedom and happiness." It must also be able to "demonstrate the adequacy of its means for obtaining this end" (135). How can anyone demonstrate any such adequacy? *Demonstration,* in the strong sense of the term, no one could claim to be able to produce. In any case, all that could be produced is an argument that establishes *the possibilities* of the desirable end of the revolution, in the way in which Lenin, Mao, and Castro demonstrated them before they began bringing about freedom and happiness. There will always be enough Herbert Mathewses around to assure us that these lovers of freedom and happiness are gentle agrarian reformers and mild liberals.

I do not intend, however, to examine *Eros and Civilization* in detail in order to substantiate my belief that it is inadmissible. I shall merely note two defects, either of which I take to be crippling: one is psychological and the other philosophical. But against the second I shall not argue explicitly either immediately or later. I shall consider it by indirection when I turn to the examination of Marcuse's hedonism. In the rest of this chapter, after examining the psychological defect, I shall make a number of remarks elicited by Marcuse's conception of the good life.

In his introduction to *Eros and Civilization,* Marcuse informs us that he uses the term *repression* in its ordinary sense. There could be no objection to this usage if he also used it in its technical, Freudian, sense and somehow managed to distinguish one usage from the other. The need for the double use and the distinction stems from the fact that *repression,* in Freud's thought, has a specific meaning and one which is closely related to another technical term, *sublimation,* from which it is distinguished. The relation between what Freud takes to be the process of repression and that of sublimation, is a complex one, and Freud himself tells us that he is not satisfied with the explanation he gives of these processes and their interrelationships. But the failure to give an adequate explanation of them does not impair the need for the distinction. Sublimation is not repression but—leaving out details—it is rather the way in which some repressed instincts find oblique or modified satisfaction. And Freud makes it clear that some forms of sublimation bring about a greater degree of satisfaction than others. In art, for instance, man's erotic tendencies find a high degree of satisfaction. While Marcuse recognizes this to be the case, he fails to give it the weight it has, because for him pleasure acquired through artistic work is acquired under the rule of the performance principle—the reality principle as it exists at any historical period—and is thus pleasure obtained under condition of repression.

If, however, we fail to distinguish between the ordinary usage of *repression* and its technical usage, the distinction between sublimation and repression in Freudian thought is erased. This is exactly what happens in *Eros and Civilization,* where Marcuse has very little to say about sublimations and what he has to say is insufficient. If the distinction between sublimation and repression is erased, all sublimations turn out to be completely unsatisfactory and no one is less insufferable than another. All civilization, then, because it is incapable of producing any satisfaction whatever, stands condemned. Let me itcrate that this primitivism is said to be the product of Reason. Nothing will do therefore except to scrap this torture and return to a state in which, re-eroticized, the whole body, and not merely a few zones, will be capable of responding to caressing. This "rational" view of human destiny does not commend itself, of course, to those—all but Marcuse and his followers—who are the victims of repression.

It is hardly necessary to point out at length that this picture of the nature of civilization is a simplistic caricature, drawn in Marcuse's usual either/or way of thinking, that is given the lie by the actualities of living under ordinary conditions in almost any period of history that can be called "normal," and that it has little to do with the experience of men living today, particularly those who live in Marcuse's hated "totalitarian democracy." Prisoners in the Isle of Pines or in Siberian concentration camps, the victims of political torture on either side of a revolution, the injured, the victims of painful illnesses—

41

this is not true of such human beings. But it is sufficiently true of the rest to give the lie to Marcuse's picture of civilization. It is true that according to Freud, and even to a realistic common sense, civilization involves ineradicable discontent—for, at least, a large number of people. But this is only one side of the coin; the other side is that living for most men, most of the time, in most periods of history, has been not only valuable but even pleasant. And when this is not the case peoples and individuals lose all hope for themselves or their children and resort to suicide. And the reason life is valuable and often pleasant is that civilization is the product, if Freud is right, of sublimation, which is not identical with repression in either sense of the term.

That normal experience yields satisfaction is not something that Marcuse denies. "In the 'normal' development," he tells us, man "is reasonably and often exuberantly happy." But in fact he is not really happy. And the reason is that "his erotic performance is brought into line with his societal [sic; the thought would have lost in depth if he had used "social"] performance." And as a result, the complying individuals reproduce more or less adequately "society as a whole." That this is of course what men want makes no difference. They should not want it. Why not? Because they ought to measure what they have against what Marcuse's "Reason" tells them they could and ought to have, and revolution will bring about.

Note in passing that no contradiction is involved in saying that life involves both discontent and value and even pleasure, for these statements are about the felt qualities of experience towards which men can have an ambivalent attitude. For Marcuse, however, the repression from which we suffer is too high a cost to pay for civilization. And since today our technology has considerably reduced the need for surplus repression, the rational thing to do would be to regress to the polymorphic condition of the child. Can all repression be done away with? Not all; some labor will be required, but not much. Civilization, therefore, should be done away with. We shall then be able to caress and fondle each other—or ourselves narcissistically or autistically—all day long. And the reason for this enticing prospect of a happy life is that all sublimation is equally insufferable repression.

This is the psychological objection to which *Eros and Civilization* is open. I pass on to consider other aspects of the book. Note, first, that Marcuse employs the word "transcendence." But he does not mean the term for a process that would be of interest to a philosopher of religion or to a metaphysician, that would take one beyond this world to a supernatural region or that could give one a glimpse of that region. What Marcuse means by "transcendence" is an utterly mundane process of development, or a transition, from repressive domination to freedom, to socialism. In such a world a man will be able to "play" and "display." On Marcuse's view there is nothing intrinsic in man that makes him want to enslave his fellows and profit from their labor. Apparently what led some men in the past to enslave their fellows was scarcity; and what keeps the enslavement going today, when scarcity need no longer be a threat, is the fact that some men are profiting from the unnecessary repression of others. The fault therefore is obviously with our institutions and these can be destroyed to make room for "rational" ones.

It is not irrelevant to notice that Marcuse does not offer either evidence or argument of any kind in favor of his hypothesis. But the hypothesis rests upon a very simple notion of man, according to which the only factor that might originally lead one man to enslave another is simply need. Is there no other factor operating? For when scarcity disappears, the enslavement is retained for the sake of profits. But what is the good of profits if there is no scarcity? They minister, the Marcusean answers, to the sense of luxury and superiority of the enslaver, they appease the sense of anonymity a man may have, and they do much else. It appears then as if the need for profit is not the only factor leading men to seek to enslave others. They do it to satisfy other needs than those created by scarcity. But for Marcuse man was born good and only scarcity led him into evil.

Thus, both Freud and Marcuse conceive of the end of man in eudaemonistic terms; but for Freud the happiness we are all supposed to crave is forever denied us, while for Marcuse we

43

could achieve it, although the social arrangements we have saddled ourselves with, successfully prevent our liberation. Marcuse tries to distinguish his view of man from that of the psychologists he calls "neo-Freudian revisionists." Revisionism of fideistic dogma, which is to say, heresy, is of course always unpardonable, unless it is practiced by oneself. But Marcuse is as much of a neo-Freudian revisionist as the psychologists he criticizes, although he is not quite as superficial as the others.

I have not attempted in these comments to "prove," in any responsible sense of the term, that Freud is closer to the truth about man than Marcuse is. I have only asserted it. Our conceptions of man belong to the discipline called by Europeans "philosophical anthropology"; they are speculative hypotheses, the product in part of our limited and idiosyncratic experience, determined by our more or less conscious goals. They are not susceptible of experimental testing. They are indeed what W. B. Gallie calls "essentially contested concepts," about which men have been arguing since they began to think and will continue to argue till the end of time. I can advance reasons for preferring Freud's notion of man to Marcuse's, although I could not do it adequately within the compass of this essay. What I can do here is further define the difference between the two writers.

WHAT SORT OF SYSTEM WOULD MARCUSE SUBSTITUTE FOR what he calls "the hell of our Affluent Society"? In *Eros and Civilization* he does not tell us enough in concrete terms about his utopia; and in *One-Dimensional Man,* employing solely the power of "negative thinking," which he advocates throughout the book, Marcuse is exclusively concerned with the detailed reasons for rejecting the world he hates. We can imagine, let me note parenthetically, that Marcuse has contempt for cliches, as one would expect a sophisticated man to have; but cliches in reverse, apparently, are not objectionable to him. "The power of positive thought" is as corny as it is inadmissible; and "the power of negative thought," used by anyone but Marcuse, would be equally corny and inadmissible; but used by him it becomes the first necessary stage in our utopian resexualization.

45

But what would his utopia, once achieved, be like? How would we live from day to day? How would relations among peoples of different languages and cultural ways of behavior be managed? Who would put out the fires, see that the game in a certain area was not overhunted, and that the rather aggressive Smiths or Joneses up the creek did not take too much of the water we need desperately if our crops are not going to die of thirst? Marcuse gives us no hint of how we would go about solving these problems. We are assured that we can become resexualized men and women. He also lays it down that the "*sensuous* rationality" that we would achieve upon gaining freedom "contains its own moral laws." (*E & C,* p. 228) The italics are in the text. In this book, therefore, he does not have to consider that were we to act on his vague hope we might find ourselves wallowing in libertinism and chaos. In one of the essays in *Negations* he asserts that man's resexualization does not lead to libertinism. But the reader of Jonas's book on the gnostics remembers the libertinism which some of the gnostic sects practiced.

In one sense, it must be allowed, the moral man makes his own decisions, and in that sense he makes his own laws. But there is another sense in which this is utterly false. We have a right therefore to ask Marcuse to give us more information than he supplies in his book about the laws that will be enacted by "*sensuous* rationality." Marcuse does not give us the smallest hint about what the laws will be or how they are contained in reborn man. Pure, unqualified negativity is what Marcuse stands for. He has no program except to blast our society. After that—who knows, except that it will be a happy society? Note that it is he himself who tells us in so many words that he has no positive program. In the last paragraph of *One-Dimensional Man* he writes:

> The critical theory of society [which is to say, Marcuse's theory] possesses no concepts which could bridge the gap between the present and the future; holding no promise and showing no success, it remains negative. (p. 257)

This is Marcuse's justification for going, with a sawed-off shotgun, after anything that moves in what he calls our "totalitarian" society, irrespective of the promise that it may contain of amelioration. Note that when he calls our society "totalitarian" he means it: we do not, according to Marcuse, live in a free world. In one of his rare sentences not wrapped up in impenetrable language, he states that "Free election of masters does not abolish the masters or the slaves." It is not possible to draw from this statement that Marcuse is an out-and-out anarchist, hoping that in his resexualized socialistic world each man will be his own master and will need no other to tell him what he should do. The power of negative thinking is so great that one cannot tell what positive thought our Great Refuser harbors in some hidden fold of his brain. For the belief that our society is totalitarian he offers the following argument:

> . . . "totalitarian" is not only a terroristic economic-technical coordination of society, but also a non-terroristic economic-technical coordination which operates through the manipulation of needs by vested interests. (*O-D M,* p. 3)

A society is totalitarian that precludes the emergence of an effective opposition to the whole, and this is satisfactorily shown by the fact that it has prevented the emergence of Marcuse's effective opposition to it. You cannot buy his books in the open market. He cannot find employment in our universities, private or public, he is not allowed to lecture anywhere, nor is his life protected by state officials when it is threatened by exasperated citizens driven to extremes by his extremism. If this is not sufficient evidence of the fact that the United States prevents the emergence of effective opposition to its repression, what kind of evidence would be acceptable?

One would have thought that the disruptive opposition to which Marcuse has given shape and guidance has been on occasions quite effective, and not only in the United States, but in Italy, Germany and France and even in Franco's Madrid.

Since he does not feel that he has been effective, this makes me assume that he measures effectiveness by a more severe standard than I do. I extrapolate to the belief that he will not feel that he has been sufficiently effective in his opposition until he sees the whole world in flames. But will his notion of effectiveness include the workers' paradise, the USSR? Will it include China and Cuba?

Marcuse also suggests that our society is totalitarian in the sense that Nazi Germany was and that Russia and China are. He writes: "Those whose life is the hell of the Affluent Society are kept in line by a brutality which revives medieval and early modern practices." (*O-D M,* p. 23) Faced with the charge, one is meant to realize how blind we all have been, with the exception of Marcuse and his followers.

But it appears there is a difference between our totalitarian society and other totalitarian societies. Some time ago I saw a newspaper item according to which Marcuse said to an audience in Italy that there actually was more freedom of speech and thought in the United States than anywhere else in the world. A pity Marcuse did not go on to examine how such an absurd paradox is possible. But of course if he went on to examine how the paradox is possible he might have to give up much of his hatred, and that is too much to ask of a "philosopher" who believes in the power of negative thought. A good definition of "philosophers," as one meets them in the academic world, is this: Philosophers are men so singleminded in the pursuit of their truths that they cannot stop to consider the evidence when that evidence goes counter to their pet prejudices.

Marcuse's refusal to give us the slightest hint of what to expect from his utopia reminds the writer of Lenin's *State and Revolution.* A notable feature of this book is that after the furious and sustained cannonade at capitalism, a pounding that left nothing standing—except the successful system of free enterprise—when towards the end of the book the time came to give at least some hints of what the classless society will be like, the society that will emerge after the dictatorship of the NKVD—or by whatever acronyms our heirs will know this institution—all Lenin had to offer was a slogan: From each according to his ability and to each according to his need. Marcuse's plan after domination withers away, and there is no more surplus repression, is no less vague: reëroticized man, after taking a few minutes daily for the labor that cannot be eliminated, will use up the rest of the day in play and display. Before signing up for the resexualization program (which I suggest we call "The Great Acceptance"), some of us who have seen or have read about how some great liberators in the past have never given their human suckers a chance—Lenin, for instance, or the Chinese Gentle Agrarian Reformers, or Mr. Herbert Mathews' mild liberal reformer, Fidel Castro—would like to know in more detail about what we will be allowed by our liberators to do. We also want to have, not the verbal assurances we have had in the past in abundance, but some objective earnest of the chances of success. Surely this is not too much to ask before we start wrecking our society and committing suicide. And why suicide? So that we can, of course, rid humanity of ourselves, who are the cancerous cells it has been afflicted by.

The ethos of our society is radically Pelagian. We cannot believe in original sin in any sense whatever, neither literally, as men in Augustine's day believed in it, nor symbolically, nor mythically. The idea of infant damnation seems to us so preposterous that we do not have a word in our language sufficiently pejorative to denigrate it with. In a broad sense Freud was an Augustinian. He was convinced that there was not much we could do to achieve happiness. His pessimism about man did not arise from a hunch, or at least it was not merely intuitive; nor was it solely the product of his temperament. His argument was grounded on his therapeutic experience. What Marcuse can put in place of Freud's pessimistic view of man is not structured by evidence, it is a creation made entirely out of his present radical frustration and his hope. But against hope there is, there can be, as I have said before, no argument.

Taken as it is intended by its author, *Eros and Civilization* is not an epoch-making book. But it is interesting for two reasons. The first is that it is another one of the many utopias—

really dystopias—peddled by unfettered dreamers in an anxious age. When we have leaned over backwards and have given the book as much or more praise than it deserves, it is also interesting as another of the many fruits of the truly seminal mind of the founder of psychoanalysis. Whether or not we should be grateful to the founder for such inedible fruit as Marcuse's book is another question.

A slight shift of standpoint reveals an important aspect of the book. We are today crowded by men who are ready to wreck our society and are intent on putting their fancies in its place. But when we take a second look at their fancies they turn out to be horrible dystopias. *Eros and Civilization* is one such. What the resexualization of man would add up to, could it be brought about, was made unambiguously explicit by Norman O. Brown in his Phi Beta Kappa oration, "Apocalypse," delivered at Columbia University and published by *Harper's* Magazine in May of 1961. Brown takes the Marcuse-Brown objective to its ultimate logical conclusion, and for the sake of "polymorphic perversity" advocates the destruction of all the values and institutions that we cherish. Instead of these, Brown would substitute play nearly all day by men who have achieved polymorphic perversity and are free from the tyranny of the genital. But for how long are we going to enjoy our play? How long would it be before Mao or his successor would have us all doing calisthenics at sunrise and marching off to work singing on an empty belly? However, for all his negativism, Marcuse is too tough an intellectual, a man too deeply steeped in Teutonic culture, to wish to pay the price Brown would not hesitate to pay for manumission from the tyranny of the genital. At any rate explicitly, Marcuse does not go as far as Brown does. The difference between them can easily be grasped by reading Marcuse's review of *Love's Body* and Brown's "reply," both published in *Negations.*

Eros and Civilization is also important because it is a milestone in the development of Marcuse's thought. It constitutes the first step taken by him in his development from a regular academic professional to the leader of the new nihilists. *Reason and Revolution* and *Soviet Marxism,* as already indicated, are the products of a man to the academic manor born. The writer is a Marxist, which means that if he is serious—and no one would want to accuse Marcuse of frivolity in this respect—given the first opportunity he would set the torch to his society. But Marxists have occupied important places in our universities since the Russian revolution. With *Eros and Civilization* Marcuse applies, so to speak, for a visa to the non-academic world. Time, circumstance, and *One-Dimensional Man,* plus the important fact that in the world he hates he enjoys freedom he would not enjoy elsewhere, finally gave him the prestigious and influential position he occupies today.

Although some conservatives have tried to deny his reputation, or more exactly his notoriety, of the fact that he is known the world over, there need be no question. He is mentioned with Mao, Trotsky, Castro and Guevara, and noticed editorially in publications like *The Times Literary Supplement* of London: he is mentioned even in Franco's country, for I have seen his views discussed and his picture reproduced three times in a magazine published in Madrid. He is a hero in France, Germany, Italy, and it goes without saying in Columbia University and points west, wherever in our world the social termites gnaw at the uprights of our civilization. The Pope and Ulbricht have referred to him by name and the Russians attack him bitterly. Nor am I speaking of the publicity he has so abundantly received since his life was threatened and he had to go into hiding. His prestige among the nihilists and his notoriety preceded the threat; indeed they were, they must have been, the cause of the threat. But in spite of his unique eminence, Marcuse is one of a type.

Why has *One-Dimensional Man* been welcomed so heartily by the new nihilists? Anyone acquainted with a few of them can answer this question with confidence. They hate our world as intensely as Marcuse, but lacking his theoretical dedication to destruction, his talent, his capacity for work, and his erudition, they hail with joy the articulation and rationalization of their emotions that the book provides them. That the rationalization is essentially histrionic and that it has been watered down to the level of their own understanding, we cannot expect them to see, since they are more histrionic than their "philosopher" and considerably more simple-minded. One has to read the book as a whole to believe how total, how unqualified, how absolute, how implacable, is Marcuse's rejection of our world. And therefore how simplistic it is. Here and there he includes a criticism of Communism. But the trick does not fool the reader. He does not hate Communism as he hates the advanced industrial democratic world of the West. This is fully confirmed by his advice in "Repressive Tolerance" that the Left be tolerated but the Right be repressed. And his hatred turns a man who was once a scholar into a disingenuous concealer of those on whose side his heart is. Thus, he calls Bertolt Brecht "a radical activist"—true enough but disingenuous, for a genuine rejection of both sides should have led Marcuse to refer to Brecht as what he truly was.

The almost tragic pathos of the new nihilism is that no one in the movement is interested in anything but "the Great Refusal." Bigotry and intolerance, raised to a philosophic principle and proclaimed virtue, hatred in the name of reason: what is all this but the arrogance of apodictic certitude claimed by fallible men? One is forced to ask the unpleasant question: What besides the gas chambers and the ovens, and the criterion used to tell their enemies, is the difference between the Nazis and their leader on the one hand, and our new nihilists and their "philosophic" leader on the other? The difference is that the Nazis ran their thousand-year Reich for less than one-and-a-half decades while Marcuse and his wreckers have not yet achieved power.

What are the charges against our society? The negative mind is indiscriminate, and some of its judgments are ridiculously petty. Mixed, the reader will find serious charges and trivial ones. To some of the serious charges we shall have to plead guilty. But as often we shall be forced to object to the exaggerated formulation of the charge and the failure to note extenuating circumstances that reduce a defect from a hideous offense to a minor crime. Marcuse takes as seriously the trivial defects as the grave ones. Some of the defects to which he objects in our culture are indeed defects, but they are defects much more obtrusive in Communist countries than in ours.

Some defects the majority of us, even the thoughtless and the uneducated, recognize for what they are, serious and in urgent need of correction, and some of them we are seeking to remedy. Some, we suspect, are afflictions of all human soci-

53

eties, large or small, and some are evils inherent in the magnificent triumph of our science and our technology. Whether these could be eliminated I do not believe anyone knows, for the only radical remedy for them would be to put a moratorium on science, and that would be suicidal. Some are petty faults. But to Marcuse all of them, great and small, are unforgivable. How any but an immature mind can find much truth in *One-Dimensional Man* is an unanswerable question. That many college students and faculty take it seriously is a symptom of our society worth pondering.

Consider one instance of Marcuse's criticism. In *One-Dimensional Man* (94), not giving Orwell credit, he spends quite a number of pages analyzing our language and condemning it. One of the criticisms he makes against it is its use of acronyms, such as NATO, SEATO, UN, AFL-CIO, and others. He allows that some of these abbreviations are "reasonable," but suggests that the abbreviations may help to repress undesired questions. Let's grant the hypothesis, although it is a statement of fact for which one cannot guess what sort of evidence could be brought to its proof or rejection. But Marcuse's tenderness to the Left leads him to forget that acronyms came into fashion with the October Revolution, and more recently, outside Russia, it was Sukarno who made the air ring with his acronyms.

Furthermore, *One-Dimensional Man* does not contain a single, sustained exercise of analysis acknowledging those forces operative in our world that offer an earnest of improvement. Nor could Marcuse have included many signs of approval, since he has a genius for showing that each and every trait we consider good is really a device of domination and enslavement. There can be no question about it: Marcuse's thought is negative criticism at its purest, in its most quintessential form. We are bad; we give no evidence whatever of a redeemable trait.

Fundamentally the argument adds up to the allegation that our society is rigged to manipulate the needs and wants of its members and to satisfy them. This is repeated in different formulations any number of times. Hence, our society is "capa-

54

ble of containing social change—qualitative change which would establish essentially different institutions, a new direction of the productive process, new modes of human existence." (*O-D M,* p. xi) You gather after some reading of Marcuse, that by "to contain" he usually means "to dam up," and not "to include." And the containment or damming up consists of our being manipulated to want what those in power force us to produce. No wonder we get what we want. But what we need and want are false needs and wants: big automobiles, hi-fi sets, split-level homes, kitchen equipment, freezers, all of them odious gadgets and devices, serving only our pseudo-happiness; for we can have them only by "the preservation of misery in the face of unprecedented wealth." (*O-D M,* p. xiii)

For some reason that remains obscure, Marcuse shares with some Americans an intense hatred for big cars. Let us follow *au pied de la lettre* one of his blasts at Detroit and its crime against humanity. He calls the blast "banal" but he offers it in all seriousness as an example of the way that the "tolerance of positive thinking is enforced tolerance—enforced not by any terroristic agency, but by the overwhelming, anonymous power and efficiency of technological society." (*O-D M,* p. 226)

Here is the blast: "The automobile is beautiful, shiny, powerful, convenient. But in a relatively short time it will deteriorate and need repair; its beauty and surface are cheap; its power unnecessary, its size idiotic, and we cannot find a parking place for it." (*O-D M,* p. 226) Banal though he calls this view, it is one he seems to be obsessed with, for in the last essay in *Negations,* published for the first time in the book, he dwells on the subject again. Along with Marcuse's outrage at our false need for big cars goes his outrage at the names of wild animals we give our cars and at the fact that, pulling up to the pump, we ask the attendant to put a tiger in the tank.

Consider first that the United States is not Madison Avenue or Detroit. The effort to appeal to Americans by giving the names of wild animals to cars cannot seriously be considered a diagnostic trait of the American ethos. In any case, it was ephemeral, and Madison Avenue and Detroit have begun to give different names to cars.

55

As to the tiger in the tank, Marcuse does not seem to realize that the picture is that of a tame and friendly tiger. But let that go. I suspect that Americans have too high a sense of the ridiculous to be caught asking to have tigers put in their tanks. And I am fully confident that no lady of refinement and education would be naive enough to make such a request. Except for unmarried graduate students, who usually ask in an apologetic voice, for a buck's worth of gas, most of the people I asked told me that they drive up to the pump and when the attendant appears they call, "Fillerup!" Marcuse's discovery is therefore more or less true: it is Detroit and Madison Avenue who try to play on the American's aggressive tendencies. But Marcuse stopped too soon: he should have gone on to inquire how well they succeeded and, to be scientific, he should have gone on to compare the aggressiveness of the Americans with that of the North Vietnamese, the Mao Red Guards, the Nazis, the Arabs and the Israelis, and the penguins of the South Pole.

Marcuse's indictment of the American's love of big cars and tigers in tanks is therefore not altogether correct. Nor is it banal —since it gives us evidence of the way Marcuse's mind works. But one truly brilliant piece of research that he conducted cannot be ignored, because it paid off magnificently. Marcuse was the first sociologist in our car-glutted world to find out that we cannot find parking spaces for our big cars. Until Marcuse proclaimed this discovery, city administrations, buildings and grounds superintendents of universities throughout the land, Boards deciding on new factory sites, churches, and even high schools, had been ignorant of the fact that Americans cannot find a place for their Caddies, Continentals, Imperials, or Rolls. Here, then, is a sociological discovery worth the acuity, the empirical savvy, the vast erudition, the alertness to living problems of our great "philosopher-sociologist." This has suggested to me that it may not have been a kook of the extreme Right or the Left who gave him seventy-two hours to vamoose from his job, but that the conspiracy probably originated in Detroit and Madison Avenue and was managed by the C.I.A. and J. Edgar. But I regretfully say I have not tested this hypothesis.

Marcuse's hatred of gadgetry and of our highly developed technology deserves further attention because it is part of what I, in my idiolect, call "the Lawrentian syndrome." Marcuse does not go as far as D. H. Lawrence did, who in all seriousness told us that the problems of our world would be solved by going back to the Elizabethans and dressing the men in gay colors (in any sense of the word "gay" you like to use) and showing their plump buttocks. But can anyone deny that there is some relationship between the hatred expressed by Marcuse and the hatred expressed by Ursula in *The Rainbow*, against machines and the men who tend them?

Although I call it "Lawrentian," I am not suggesting that Lawrence originated it. It is part of a strong counter current in our world, and one to which Jacques Ellul did not give sufficient weight. That it is idiosyncratic and arbitrary can be seen by the fact that the technophobes so frequently choose different objects or aspects of our world to hate. That it is strong, that it seems to be increasing, and that it has probably been a counter-factor in the development of human culture since the first savage saw the advantage of chipping the first stone, are matters about which I guess. There seems to be, one almost dares to say, a genetic Luddite strain in mankind, more likely to burst into an epidemic in our world of overwhelming and even threatening machines than in the world of technically clever men who have lacked or lack knowledge of physics and engineering. I am of the conviction—for what it may be worth —that once man chipped the first stone, he was on the road to atomic energy and space exploration. It was hard and very slow going at first. In the last fifty years the going can only be compared to a tidal wave, or one of the great rivers of the earth in full flood. Remember that Faraday was asked—I do not remember by whom or when—of what use was the induction coil, and he replied to the effect that it was a rather interesting but useless machine.

Note also that Marcuse is a sociologist and a student of psychology who leaves out of account in his rage at our silly need for big cars, the fact that it is but a new variant of a very ancient human weakness. Man has always suffered from a pathetic

57

need to give outward proof of his superiority over his fellows. The late Eighteenth Century or early Nineteenth did not have big Rolls Royces or Lincolns, but to the annoyance of Emma Woodhouse, Augusta Elton boasted of her sister's landau-farouche. A human weakness, universally known by moralists for God knows how long, it constitutes the brilliant discovery in our period by the sociologists who naturally proceeded to tag it with a high-sounding name. A big car is an indispensable status symbol. A man possessing a bit of knowledge of his fellow men, and one expects more than a bit of knowledge from a writer who is a "philosopher" and a "sociologist," would pity the human animal who today bases his self-respect on the size of his car, just as he would pity the Spaniard in Venezuela who, a couple of centuries ago, measured the depth of his dignity by the height of the cane he was allowed by law to carry, or would pity the Chinese, who measured his by the length of his nails and the crushed feet of his wife and concubines. Nor is the status-symbol mentality one recently acquired by man. I am no historian of human fatuity, but it is interesting to note that when the Goths conquered Spain, those who could built villas in the Roman fashion and displayed their mastery of Latin. This was the way the big wheels among them displayed—forgive me for using the term—"status symbols." The male Taureg, to mention another case, wears a veil. This practice may have originated in the fact that the litham protects the head and face against desert sandstorms. But I have read somewhere that today its importance is largely one of status. Neither women nor young men wear veils. And the importance of a man is measured by his refusal to remove the veil. But it is not the litham alone that functions as status symbol: apparently the color of the veil distinguishes the high from the low-born.

Another example of the apparently universal need men have had for status symbols is their silly concern with genealogy. The chroniclers of the Tudor monarchy, J. H. Plum has recently noticed, were eager to trace the unbroken succession of their monarchs back to the Conquest, to Alfred, and even to David and Adam himself. One last example. Francis Huxley records that he was told in Haiti that a chamber-pot is a mark of respectability. He was informed that when a young woman goes on a journey, she'll take her private pillow with her, stuffed with down, and a chamber pot for all to see. Huxley never saw the sight, and comments: "I felt somehow cheated, as if one more ancient courtesy had decayed, and the country had lost another opportunity to behave with style." It is a pity if the custom has been lost, for it seems an excellent means for young ladies to display their status.

I am confident that Margaret Mead may know another tribe (other than the Arapesh) in which the equality, the modesty, the refusal to stand out from the rest deprives a man of any way of indicating his superiority over his fellows. But shall we say that this drive is the norm in human groups?

Why are we called *one-dimensional* men? I do not remember any passage in the book by that name in which Marcuse gives us an explicit and detailed explanation of his term. But I gather from a number of discussions in his book (for instance, one on p. 15) that we men of today lost one dimension our ancestors had, because our affluent society has so manipulated us that we can no longer notice the difference, as our ancestors could, between the actual state of hell in which we live and the heaven we could turn this hell into if we allowed Marcuse to guide us to his dystopia. There is also a section in Chapter 4 of *One-Dimensional Man* entitled "The Research of Total Administration" (p. 104) that tells us that we have redefined the function and content of thought, and thus we have reduced the tension between thought and reality by weakening "the power of negative thought." Much sooner than Huxley anticipated, our society has turned into *Brave New World*.

I do not believe that Marcuse mentions Aldous Huxley's dystopia, but what revolts us about the pseudo-humans of 632 AF, animals that look like us but do not seem to have much in common with us, is what revolts Marcuse about ourselves. According to Marcuse, the only way to be human, is to be negative and to yearn for resexualization. Hence for destruction. And after that, in the midst of the charred rubble and the half-burnt corpses, we shall play and display.

IN *One-Dimensional Man* WE COME ACROSS SOME WACKY hypotheses and theories, each one of which would have to be thoroughly examined were we engaged in an exhaustive investigation of the thought of our negative prophet. I shall restrict my efforts to the examination of two instances of Marcuse's thought that refer to subjects about which I am not altogether ignorant. I urge the reader, however, to take them as examples of many theories that he will find in this book.

Let me first turn to Marcuse's view of the function of art. He writes:

> Prior to the advent of this cultural reconciliation, literature and art were essentially alienation, sustaining and protecting the contradiction—the unhappy consciousness of the divided

world, the defeated possibilities, the hopes unfulfilled, and the promises betrayed. They were a rational, cognitive force, revealing a dimension of man and nature which was repressed and repelled in reality.

He concludes the following paragraph with these words:

> But art has its magic power only as the power of negation. It can speak its own language only as long as the images are alive which refuse and refute the established order. (*O-D M,* pp. 61-2)

It should be noted, but only in passing, that Marcuse has been charged with a confusion, if not outright contradiction, regarding the role of art. For in an essay written in 1937 and published in *Negations,* "The Affirmative Nature of Culture," he would have it that "Ideal beauty was the form in which yearning could be expressed and happiness enjoyed." He also tells us that, "Unlike the truth of theory, the beauty of art is compatible with the bad present, despite and within which it can afford happiness." And finally that, "By exhibiting the beautiful as present, art pacifies rebellious desire." But in spite of the weight given this matter by Paul A. Robinson in *The Freudian Left* (New York, Evanston and London, 1969, p. 183) if there is a contradiction, it cannot be held to be a serious one, since the thesis Marcuse seems intent on defending, not merely in *One-Dimensional Man* but elsewhere, is that "art has this magic power only as the power of negation." It is to this thesis that I turn in the following pages.

What Marcuse is saying is that the function of art is cognitive and that the knowledge it gives is knowledge of those aspects of man and his world that do not yet exist but ought to have existed at the time the art was made. What art does, then, is to condemn by contrast. The artist shows men the ideal and by contrast men discover their actual plight. But isn't this a kind of Platonic aesthetics in reverse? For Plato's objection to the poets was that they did not represent the ideal and pictured the gods as a scurrilous lot. Marcuse does not agree with Plato.

61

He says the artist pictures the ideal, and by contrast he shows up the existing reality. Could the problem be settled by authority, I would quote Nietzsche against Marcuse, for the mad German is undoubtedly a much better judge on questions of art than our atrabilious ex-Berliner. I would particularly urge that the reader look closely at Nietzsche's notion of the yea-saying power of tragedy. But the question is—as important questions usually are—one in which fact and theory are in close interrelationship.

We need not doubt that Marcuse means exactly what he says, for considerably later in the book (p. 238) he writes: "Like technology, art creates another universe of thought and practice against and within the existing one." Notice, always *against*, never *for*.

Let us look into Marcuse's theory. It would have made it easier for us to be fair to it if we had been told how far back to date the era of "cultural reconciliation." For in many of the great ages of modern civilization, since the Elizabethan in England or the Golden Age in Spanish literature and art, makers have made art that celebrates and affirms "the matter of experience" that the maker was able to "in-form" into "the substance of art," and art has always been taken—and justifiedly so—to celebrate life, to affirm life fully. In literature the art of the unhappy consciousness of the divided world, the defeated possibilities, the hopes unfulfilled, and the promises betrayed, did not begin until recently. In English literature, it followed the great achievement of Henry James. Since then, we have had a literature of renunciation, a bitter critique of the world we live in, from, say, D. H. Lawrence to the dried-up ordure that goes for literature today. But since even in our own society of cultural reconciliation some artists have made objects that are paeans to the beauty of woman, to the lovely delicacy of a child, to the cheerful brilliance of a bouquet of flowers, Marcuse finds it necessary to put his conception of the function of art beyond the possibility of factual validation. The job is easy. He shifts the focus of attention without warning his reader about what he is doing. The artist may think he is celebrating reality and the listener or spectator may agree with the artist.

But that is irrelevant. What matters is that the created object negates the repressive actuality.

> The decisive distinction is not the psychological one between art created in joy and art created in sorrow, between sanity and neurosis, but that between the artistic and the societal reality. The rupture with the latter, the magical or rational transgression, is an essential quality of even the most affirmative art. . . . Art contains the rationality of negation. (*O-D M*, p. 63)

Marcuse seems to mean that all art without exception carries within itself the rationality of negation. I guess that it is to be taken for granted that all negation is rational, even if it should negate Kant's famous proposition that five plus seven make twelve.

Thus Marcuse has put his assertion beyond the reach of criticism. It can't be touched. But can't it? Let me first note that no sophisticated critic today, whatever his views on the so-called "intentional fallacy," would fail to distinguish the intentions and resources of the artist from the product of his efforts. The psychological question is therefore not at issue. Marcuse's decisive distinction is a red herring. When we turn to his view of the function of art, we find Marcuse making an assertion that would call for proof from a lesser man. The object—the novel or play, the canvas—may seem to celebrate the events about which it is: the nude, the dancing couple, or the tender child. But what it actually does is to reveal a dimension—his term, of course—of man, society, or the universe, that we have repressed: defeated possibilities, unfulfilled hopes, betrayed promises. How does Marcuse prove that this is true of all art throughout the ages until our own day? Does he need proof? Isn't it sufficient for him to assert it? But on what grounds does he assert it? The answer, I suggest, is that what he has done is to deduce his view of the function of art from his conviction that our society and all past societies have needed and still need change. Once in possession of his deduction, and without any regard for the facts whatever, he applies it to all art. But how did he arrive at his view of our society if he did not do so

63

empirically? This is a double-barrelled question that I cannot stop to consider at this point, but to which I shall give some attention later. For Marcuse is and is not an empiricist, and an extensive consideration of exactly what method he uses is of some importance, since it transcends the problem of Marcuse and his nihilism. Postponing this matter, it is enough here to note that throughout this book Marcuse manipulates the facts to feed his hatred. *One-Dimensional Man* is not science; among other things it is self-expression.

Let us consider Marcuse's aesthetics further. We know that towards the end of his life Renoir painted in actual physical pain and that the glorious period of Van Gogh's career, the pitiful five years or so that he lived after he arrived in Paris and moved south, was a period in which he lived in Hell. His letters and the accounts we have are a record of intense personal suffering. Both Renoir's arthritis and Van Gogh's mental illness and poverty were no doubt the malignant product of "societal" repression. I have no other evidence for this statement than Marcuse's basic thesis from which I have deduced it. But in spite of the fact that both men were the victims of ruthless "societal" repression, to spectators generally their canvases seem fully affirmative. The Frenchman loved the sensuous beauty of anything his eyes rested on, and his eyes rested with peculiar delight on the lovely sensuality of woman, the joyfulness of the world around him, and the gaiety of nature. There are canvases in which his love of the world threatens almost to step beyond celebration and to become a sentimental or even a saccharine view of it. One thinks of so many canvases where the threat makes itself felt but the mastery of the artist, his control of color and composition, holds the threat up just in time. In any case, the great majority of Renoir's canvases seem to be a riot of color and affirmation; it was the bourgeois world into which Renoir climbed by the strength of his talent, although of course we must not lose sight of the fact that it was the world that repressed him. The canvases of the mad Dutchman celebrate the vibrant glory of flowers, of cypresses, of a flock of ravens flying low over a field of wheat ready for harvest, and even the singular attractiveness of a cheap chair—a chair that had to be creatively seen by Van Gogh to reveal its quality to us.

But we are wrong if that is what we see in the work of Renoir or Van Gogh. Neither painter celebrated the actual world. Renoir did not apprehend creatively the sensuous loveliness of living women, the tenderness of children, the glory of flowers. Van Gogh did not discern creatively the vibrant nervousness of cypresses, the dark, living radiance of ravens flying over wheatfields, nor the splendor that made men call the helio- tropic blossom of *Helianthus annus,* "the sunflower." What these two activists, fighting at the cultural front against "soci- etal" repression, actually did was to externalize on canvas their Platonic dreams of perfection, suggested to them by the ugly, frigid, enervated humanity and arid world that surrounded them: the skinny, starved young hags with pendulous breasts, the pot-bellied, skinny, starving children, the stunted, "societ- ally" repressed flowers, needing water and a little manure that our "societal" domination denied them. But since society re- presses all of us, except Marcuse and his nihilistic followers, we ask how those two men, the Frenchman and the Dutchman, managed to join the thin red line, or more precisely put, the all-too-thick line of reds, that make up the elite corps of the Great Refusers? Marcuse did not consider it worthwhile to supply us with an explanation. But we have a right to ask for one, because if society is as repressive of men, women, chil- dren, cypresses and sunflowers as Marcuse says it is, it would be of the greatest and most imperative urgency to know how the "philosopher" of nihilism and his shills escaped the crip- pling domination that damages the rest of us. Who knows? Some of us might try the tricks by which Marcuse and his nihilists escaped, and a few of those who try them might pull it off.

But it is possible that my remarks are totally irrelevant. Could it be that the sensual Frenchman and the mad Dutchman came before the age of cultural reconciliation? This is the reason that it is necessary to know when that age began. Did it begin after Maillol? Or after Matisse?

65

But this is not all. Sometimes it is convenient for Marcuse to further strengthen the impregnability of his irrefutable theory. It then turns out that the role of art is not only to present to us by contrast the evil of our world, but also to imitate the actual evil in its full unredeemable squalor, ugliness, and futility. At one such time he wrote: "The real face of our time shows in Samuel Beckett's novels." (*O-D M,* p. 247) One wonders. In Beckett's novels only, and not in Céline? But Céline was a fascist. It may be hard on many critics to reconcile Céline's antisemitism and his collaboration with the Germans, with the fact that he is a great writer, an artist of real stature —even though his vision of the world is just as acerbic, but in a different way, as Beckett's, or Marcuse's.

The introduction of Beckett's work can be interpreted as allowing cognizance of an important genre—if that is what it is—of literature and art. It allows us to include Hogarth, Daumier, and Swift: the satirists, in short, in literature or in graphic art. Unfortunately for Marcuse's argument, the introduction of this kind of art erases the either/or distinction between days prior to cultural reconciliation and our own age. But there is still another sense in which Marcuse's theory of art over-simplifies the data any such theory should take account of. What can we do with Rabelais? Here is a man well acquainted with the folly of mankind. But it did not outrage him: it amused him. And there is one more sense in which Marcuse's tendency towards simple disjunction leads him to overlook important data—which considered would have made his distinction between art of negation and art of cultural reconciliation more complex: I mean, a man like Goya.

We cannot simply say that Goya falls under what we may call —for convenience—Marcuse's first account of the function of art. As Marcuse would have it, Goya could be said to present ideal alternatives to the world in which he lived. The two *Majas* are sufficient evidence but considerably more could be brought forward if needed. And he seems "to present the real face of [his] time," in *Los Caprichos* and in *Los Desastres de la Guerra.* Marcuse's grand over-simplification about the function of art makes no allowance for the heterogeneity of the

66

objects made, which is the result of an often changing response of the artist to his world. The theory ignores the complex moods of the artist, his sometimes radical ambivalence, the attraction and repulsion with which the world, sometimes simultaneously and often in sequence, makes him shuttle back and forth between incompatible attitudes. In Goya's case, the artist began his career with great success, much in demand. He ended in exile, living in total silence, pain, rejection. The Eighteenth Century faith he had in reason was totally lost. A full life had eroded it. But Goya, both man and artist, shows how empty are the wholesale oversimplifications of Marcuse's notion of the function of art.

There is no need to argue further that Marcuse's theory of the function of art was not derived from a humble consideration of the heterogeneity of the phenomenon throughout Western history. What it gives evidence of is the readiness of the nihilist to press anything he can lay his hands on to his end. For him all pegs, round or square, fit his all-purpose revolutionary hole. The world presented in the canvas of an artist may be a world of sensuous women, of lovely landscapes, of flaming sunflowers and cypresses pushing toward heaven with their energy. But Marcuse declares that the artist does not show what is but what ought to be. However, when the product of the artist's work moans with despair, pain, futility, emptiness, anguish, when it overpowers us with the stench of human beings living in garbage cans, then, but only then, does the artist show the true face of his time.

Marcuse is a very fortunate man. He has the felicity of having achieved what the rest of us cannot even aspire to reach. We are burdened with respect for facts and inhibited by a sense of fairness, and we feel hesitation and anxiety before complex problems. Marcuse is not burdened with any such handicaps. He is not baffled by the world in which he lives. It is all very simple: our world is hell. In view of this fact, the artist cannot celebrate the world. All he can do is condemn it by contrast or paint it as it is. Marcuse is able to advance apodictic ideas, and since they are apodictic, criticism cannot reach them. If he suspects that there are facts that contradict his views he simply reverses the direction of his thought, asserts another undeniable fact, and shrugs his shoulders at the effect that this new assertion may have on his older views. He has it going and coming. Facts? Anyone who knows anything knows that facts must be interpreted to be facts—or rather that the data that offers itself to us must be interpreted into facts. Facts are congealed hypotheses. If the data must be interpreted, why not interpret it to reinforce *my* prejudices? Logic? Coherence? Not in our affluent society. Not if they interfere with our aim: to wreck it. All we have a right to expect in this hell is the domination of our masters and the negations of our savior. T. H. Huxley said that Herbert Spencer's idea of a tragedy was a hypothesis slain by a fact. The hypotheses of the other Herbert, Marcuse, are so levitated into the blue yonder that they cannot be slain by facts. No facts can reach them. How could it be otherwise? Marcuse's thoughts are the hypotheses of a man who plays the game of heads-I-win-tails-you-lose. Thus, it is not as difficult always to be right as we repressed men think.

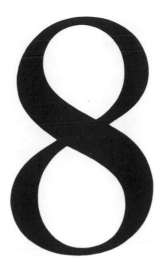

I CANNOT TAKE UP *au fond* THE TECHNICAL REASONS THAT
"vitiate"—to use another of Marcuse's favorites—his theory of
the cognitive function of art. I have written on the problem
several times, and those interested in my views on the subject
can easily find them. Here I shall have to be content with a
summary of some of the reasons that seem to me to make
Marcuse's view inadmissible. Let me begin with the fact that
in actuality art serves a multitude of heterogeneous functions,
some of which are incompatible with others. Thus, according
to the greatest of Greek philosophers, Homer and his kind did
nothing but tell impious and scurrilous tales about the gods;
they chose to be liars when they should have given men
glimpses of absolute beauty— the perfect circle—absolute
truth—the idea of the Good, according to Plato's philosophy,

I guess—absolute holiness, and absolute goodness. To his pupil (whom many students of philosophy believe to have been a greater man than his teacher) art, if we can do what aestheticians and critics have been doing for twenty-three centuries, generalize from the *Politics* and the *Poetics,* had two functions: its first function was to imitate, because men like imitations; the second function was to drain the two humors, pity and fear, that collect in the soul as bile collects in Frenchmen's livers. We must occasionally physic ourselves. Aristotle also held that poetry is more true than history. So art was cognitive, but not of the ideal, as Plato thought it should be, but, I guess, of actuality. For the Philosopher, it is clear, when a tragedy is well made—which is to say, when made according to his mechanical rules—it does what it is supposed to do: It pleases us, it physics us, and it tells the truth. For I. A. Richards—to jump from the peaks of antiquity to the sea level of the present—verse is a substitute for religion; a view which, if I remember correctly, was earlier held by Carlyle. Although Richards changed his mind since he propounded his scientistic theory in *Principles of Literary Criticism,* I wouldn't doubt that there are a number of learned professors for whom poetry still serves the function Richards ascribed to verse and art in general. When *Principles* was first published, a large number of professors took to his theory as cows in pasture take to the man who brings them salt. But Richards is today, as Venezuelans say, "history." Learned professors today light candles before other altars. Timothy Dwight, on the other hand, told his undergraduates in Chapel that Shakespeare's plays were the language of vice and the theatre was gross and immoral. Dwight was saving souls at Yale in 1804. And Dwight's view of the function of art (generalizing what he said about Shakespeare) was once orthodox doctrine in New England and is still held by some academics in our day—one of whom told me once that pictures of nudes were for bedrooms: ageing Asians, it is known, prefer ground rhinoceros's horn. Of course people who have found the right location for nudes are not interested in art. Neither are the undergraduates one still runs across who tell you that the purpose of art is self-expression: on the assumption, natural to our participatory democracy, that undergraduates have very important emotions and ideas to express. Art dealers, producers and, of late, shrewd investors, know that art can be made to perform a totally different function. In Aristophanes, Aeschylus and Euripides agree with the Russian Shoe-banger (USSR, Ret.) about the function of art. In *The Frogs,* the two Greeks agree that the function of the theatre is to improve civic virtue, and the Russian held, when he had the power to shoot off his mouth about things that he knew and that he did not, that the function of art was to create enthusiastic slaves for his system.

We must not forget that art is a three-letter word that covers a vast territory. It includes the work of Giotto, Titian, Bosch, Grunewald, El Greco, Goya, Daumier, and Pascin. It also includes Homer, Aeschylus and Sophocles, Dante, the Elizabethans, Calderón, Tirso, and Jane Austen, Céline and Beckett, and that "radical activist" Brecht, and works like *Justine, Tropic of Cancer* and *Naked Lunch.* It includes the work of Bach and his glorious successors, also of Vivaldi, Bocherini, and the others. It includes Chartres and a little jewel of Gothic architecture with which Marcuse must be very well acquainted, the Freiburg Cathedral. One has to have seen it to appreciate in full how precisely its builders expressed, through one of its gargoyles, their impudent acceptance of life. It includes Frank Lloyd Wright. It includes so much else that I could not, did I desire to do it, give an instance of each class. To decide what is the purpose of art we must not only look into the ways it has been used but into the heterogeneity of objects that have been called "art." As a fact, art performs whatever purpose it happens to perform for those who have commerce with it—unless we show, by means of adequate and detailed analysis, and with an alert third ear to the nuances, that the picture the dealer sells and the investor buys is not art, although if someone else were to buy it for his aesthetic delight it would then be art. It is not impossible to accomplish this feat by means of the properly nuanced distinctions. Let me be emphatic: it can be done. But no one who has read a few pages of the prophet of the new nihilists would accuse him of being moved by concern for nuances. All that the power of negative thought can do is to negate.

What ought the purpose of art to be? How should we use art in order to use it as art and not as something else? We are no better off when we leave description and move to prescription, when we pass from the merely empirical enumeration of the multitude of usages to which art is actually put, to the enumeration of the usages to which it ought to be put, for there are as many views about its proper usage as there are aestheticians worth their salt.

In order to deal with this problem with the seriousness and adequacy it demands, I believe we must draw a fundamental distinction, in the absence of which our efforts to decide what the function of art ought to be are likely to go wrong; or if they go right, they will do so by a lucky guess, and no philosopher can rest content with such a guess and retain his self-respect. In order to deal properly with the normative function of art we must distinguish between the residential function of art and the non-residential functions—in the singular and the plural respectively. Without this distinction we have no means of deciding whether anyone who wishes to call art any old thing that he happens to be interested in for any old reason that occurs to him, is right or wrong. But kindly note that I am discussing theoretical matters; I am arguing for what seems to me to be an important theoretical foundation on which our criticism and our conception of the relation of art to other modes of human activity must be grounded if we are to avoid wallowing in confusion or hitting off the right answer by luck.

It is neither surprising nor astonishing to find that the great majority of critics crave for, and actually indulge in, unfettered freedom from the rigorous limitations that theory imposes on criticism—or should impose on it. They hate the restrictiveness of theory. They want to say, for instance, that art purveys knowledge, or "is for" certain religious values, just as the Shoe-banger would have it that art "ought" to disclose the glories of socialist reality. Restrictions are not for the majority of critics.

They are exempt from the limitations of logic; they have a better instrument to accomplish their tasks, eloquence. Critics would rather roam the unfenced prairies, like wild *manadas,* than live respectable lives in well-fenced corrals and do an honest day's work with a logically controlled, coherent system in the saddle. Ah, the freedom of the untamed stallion. Utter nonsense, of course, which they would be ashamed of if they abandoned their eloquence for a minute or two and stopped to think that it does not take a wild stallion long to produce a wild *manada* of runts useless for anything but canned dog meat.

I have not forgotten that recently the freedom for which our critics crave and in which they have all along indulged without benefit of apologetics, has been justified for them by the new evangel. Know the truth and the truth will make you free. The "repressive" limitations I am advocating are the result of my not having heard that the concept "art" is an open concept. But I had known it all along, I did not need to hear it from a Wittgensteinian. All that is new to the dictum is the moniker. Given the ethos of our day, the moniker is an honorific one. We do not need an extensive knowledge of the history of art to know that art is indeed and has always been what is now called an open concept. Until the new evangel brought the old knowledge back to us in a new language we knew well enough that new art, when first presented, is often fought bitterly and declared to be not art. Once the new art gains acceptance, it becomes entrenched and denies still newer art the honorific title of art

But it is the concept that is open. And critics do not write criticism of concepts; they write about this actual book, called a novel. But offered problems of form and substance they had never had to face before, they write about these paintings, these pieces of carved wood or welded railings, this strange "score" that produces only what to their trained ears sounds like shocking noises. In order to decide whether any of these new shocking objects are or are not art the Wittgensteinian is of no help to them but rather a hindrance. If art is an open concept anything whatever that anyone wants to call art is indeed art. But to carry on their jobs—however conceived—

critics must close their concepts. They have no alternative if they are to stay above the minimum degree of tolerable clarity. If they leave the concept open they have to face an unpleasant dilemma: either they have to examine anything thrown at them, or at least allow that anything thrown at them is worthy of examination, or they have to quit and go fishing. Too many critics refuse to face the dilemma.

I shall cite my favorite instance of a critic who has produced work of some distinction—in many respects of genuine distinction, but in others of merely specious distinction—with an open concept of the novel: F. R. Leavis. While he does not allow that C. P. Snow is a novelist—with which judgment I heartily concur, for we must distinguish between reportage and imaginative creation—he would have it, as I have pointed out before, that Lawrence, in his novels—or, more precisely, in his "novels"—is a great artist, a healer of his own wounded soul and the souls of others, a social historian, a great humorist, and I forget how many more great and wonderful things. But Leavis is able to produce work of distinction because first, the works that are the objects of his critical attention have already been selected for him by previous critical acclaim and, second, because his critical insights about well recognized artistic objects are often penetrating. And this is the case in spite of the nonsense he may peddle about the health-giving qualities and the historical achievements of that sick idol of his who never was able to heal himself.

The residential function defines art; if the object does not perform the function it is not art—*under the definition,* of course. The non-residential functions that art may perform and that it is often found performing, give rise to the question whether an object that performs some of them is art or is something else—again, *under the given definition.* This is not a question that can be taken up in this essay. But I cannot refrain from noting that the discordant babel of criticism in all the arts stems, not so much from the mutually incompatible notions of what art is, as from a much more radical source, from the critics' failure to stipulate explicitly their basic notions of what art is and how it functions.

74

Before taking up the important question of how Marcuse decided what was the function of art, let me note in passing that with different goals and a different scale of values, Marcuse's conception of the function of art is not different, formally, from the conceptions, implicit at least, that guide the work of satirists and cartoonists, as well as such distinguished aestheticians as the Shoe-banger, Timothy Dwight of Yale, and the Aeschylus and the Euripides of Aristophanes. There are between these and others of their kind, material differences as to the function of art. But formally they all agree. American Stalinists—if the expression be not a contradiction in terms—when their voices were heard in the land during the Thirties, would have had no difficulty agreeing with Marcuse, as much as they disliked him on political grounds. But while Stalinists outside the borders of the Sacred Motherland encourage satirists and cartoonists, so long as their work is directed against the world in which they live, within the sacred precincts of the Motherland they would deal as promptly and efficiently with a Goya, or a Daumier, or a Swift, as they deal with any negative thinker or maker.

We are, at long last, ready for the important question: How did Marcuse decide what is the function of art? Although I believe that I have plodded through the whole of Marcuse's available writings relevant to this question, I do not remember where he has made the proper analysis to show how he can move from the multitude of actual functions that art performs to the function he believes art ought to perform. In the absence of a clarification from him, I shall permit myself, with diffidence, the luxury of a guess. But before I make it let me insist with some emphasis that my criticism is not that Marcuse has not made the identical analysis I have sketched here to arrive at the conclusion I would arrive at, before he decides what ought to be the function of art. He could have—and has a perfect right to have—reached his own conclusion in a way that seems the proper way. My point is that he has not seen the problem at all. He has simply asserted what he, according to his needs, demands from art, and art has given to him according to its abundant capacity. We have seen that if we stay at the

75

descriptive level, art's capacity to perform all sorts of disparate functions seems to be unlimited. The followers of Marcuse are not people concerned with close-woven thinking, with tight arguments, explicit definitions, and rigorous categorial schemes. They are quite happy with his asseverations. They do not stop to ask for the indispensably thorough analysis that would be required firmly to ground his negations in the bedrock of theory. Below I shall show that years before writing *One-Dimensional Man,* Marcuse had taken up at their required depth some problems that in the bible of the new nihilists he merely asserts *ex cathedra.* But I am not acquainted with a discussion in depth by him of the difficult problem of the function of art.

THE OTHER INSTANCE OF MARCUSE'S THOUGHT THAT I PRO-
pose to examine is his quarrel with Anglo-American, so-called
linguistic, or analytic, philosophy. Because it is not easy to
share Marcuse's enthusiasm for a cliche in reverse, "the power
of negative thinking," it is a pleasure to report that some of
Marcuse's criticisms of linguistic philosophizing are well taken,
they are shrewd and valid points, some of them fresh, some not
at all negative, some important, and some possess considerable
damaging power. I do not agree with Marcuse about what he
takes the role of philosophy to be: his views on this matter are
as arbitrary and unhistorical as his view of the function of art.
But one must agree with much of what he says about Wittgenstein and Austin—who, taken together with Ryle and their well
indoctrinated parrots, I think of as "The Club."

As was the case with my examination of Marcuse's views on art, my discussion of Marcuse's criticism of linguistic philosophy cannot be exhaustive. I shall dwell only on those of Marcuse's criticisms that are of interest to me. But I cannot let myself be drawn into a minute analysis of technical details. Technicalities are indispensable for a well-grounded philosophical critique. Unfortunately they are of interest only to professionals.

Some of the criticisms Marcuse makes of analytic philosophy have been made by many of us in the classroom and in writing, although of course from diverse standpoints, and therefore from standpoints that exclude one another. In particular Ernest Gellner's book, *Words and Things,* should be mentioned, for it is a sustained critical analysis of this type of philosophizing. Indeed it was so demolishing a job that Ryle, at the time of its publication editor of *Mind*—The Club's house organ—refused to have it reviewed in its pages. Let me say, parenthetically, that we must be grateful to Ryle for giving us a concrete demonstration of the quality of open-mindedness and attention to criticism that distinguishes some contemporary philosophy. This is the way "to do philosophy." You do others in, but when anyone rises up in criticism of your views you deny him a hearing: a very effective way of keeping your dogmas intact and your disciples in line.

One of Marcuse's attacks on Wittgenstein, Austin, Ryle, and their yes-yes disciples will be found by some of Marcuse's readers to be amusing but not at all damaging. Marcuse writes:

> Austin's contemptuous treatment of the "alternatives" to the common usage of words, and his defamation of what we "think up in our armchairs of an afternoon"; Wittgenstein's assurance that philosophy "leaves everything as it is"—such statements exhibit, to my mind, academic sado-masochism, self-humiliation, and self-denunciation of the intellectual whose labor does not issue in scientific, technical or like achievements (*O-D M,* p. 173).

The weakness of this kind of dismissal—the most obvious weakness, for it has several and it is a dismissal, not a disproof—is that it is a game that two can play, and no one need lose if he has time, energy, and his wits about him. It's a game fit for the proverbial fishwives of London Town. There is nothing easier than "defaming," as Marcuse would put it, the opposition, by flushing it down the psychoanalytic water closet. And there is nothing less rewarding—intellectually, that is; for emotionally there are few things some people find more pleasant than to out-fish-wife an opponent. Let me give you an example. Suppose a critic traces my argument to a mental disorder from which he says I am suffering. Let him call me, for example, a sado-masochist. I move against him in four steps: One, "So I am a sado-masochist, am I?", I ask with a sneer. Two, "As for the 'sado', you have no evidence, for the women I have loved have been ladies and won't talk." Step three, "As for the 'masochist', I plead guilty. The evidence? The pain I have inflicted on myself reading Marcuse." With four I go on the offense and wind up: "You, Sir, foul the air with your intellectual droppings. You are afflicted with a severe case of intellectual encopresis. Your move . . ." But neither he nor I can prove anything except who can best the other in the very useless game of fish-wifing the opposition. Since this kind of game is usually initiated solely for subjective reasons and usually arises from a sense of impotence, it is never ruled by a decent attitude towards logic or fact. The absence of rules enables the contenders to carry on and on for as long as they can take it or dish it out. The first man who has to go loses.

A criticism that is made by Marcuse that is damaging to the logophiliacs has been frequently made before, in varying formulations: The goals that this kind of philosophizing sets for itself are not worth the social resources spent in carrying it out. What the members of "the Club" are doing is trivial and sometimes frivolous. On this point Marcuse has a number of devastating remarks to make. He goes about his effective job of demolition in the following manner. He gives a long quotation from Austin's *Other Minds* and concedes that Austin's analysis is probably unsurpassable in its exactitude and clarity. "But that is all it is," he comments, and goes on to assert that "not only is it not enough but that it is destructive of philosophical thought and of critical thought as such."

I shall invert Marcuse's order. What critical thought *as such* means is anyone's guess. To me it does not mean a thing. But drop the "as such" and Marcuse's criticism is valid. We do not have to accept Marcuse's notion of "the historical task of philosophy" to agree with him that the logophiliacs' notions of philosophizing are destructive of philosophical thought. Marcuse's point that analytic philosophy is destructive of philosophy, as he goes on to develop it, introduces a consideration that, so far as my acquaintance with the literature on analytic philosophy goes, seems to me to be not only important but original. The clarity sought by analytic philosophers cannot be achieved by means of ordinary language. To achieve it they must use language, and the language they must use, in respect to the ordinary speech to be clarified, is a meta-language. This is acknowledged by the linguistic analysts, but they believe they can do the job with the same language that they are criticizing. Ordinary language can be used both as the object of analysis and as meta-language. But Marcuse points out that ordinary language cannot be analyzed with ordinary language functioning as a meta-language. To clarify ordinary discourse a technical vocabulary is needed.

In fact the avoidance of technical terminology is not successful. Take a phrase like "category mistakes," or the term "dilemma" or the notion of "logical oddity"—none of these terms can be understood by a man who has a college education unless he took courses with members of the Club. But their precise meaning (assuming that they have such a meaning, something which does not hold for the notion of "logical oddity") is no part of the ordinary language of anyone unless he has done time in an English university or the American academic colonies. These terms are thus part of a technical vocabulary. Furthermore, who speaks ordinary language? I recently ran into a worker who had some high school education and did not understand the word "vertical" or the expression "a surface at right angles to another." My ordinary language was not his; and I am certain that when he gossips with his wife or talks to his fellow workers, he uses a language that is not intelligible to me. Indeed, the language of college students outside the classroom —interspersed at the moment in the middle West with a nasal sound or two per sentence, something like, "Yoonoh?" meaning, I guess, "Do you know?"—is today, to me, not easily followed, although when I began teaching I had no trouble with it. I am saying that the notion of ordinary language is as confused as it is confusing, unless the context is made explicit. Ordinary language of what group? Of the blacks in Curaçao who speak *papiamento?* Or of those in Surinam who talk *taki-taki?* Or of those who have done time in an English university? Or in an English academic colony in the United States?

I do not intend to suggest that Marcuse advocates that we should be resigned to live in a perpetual intellectual fog. In any case such advocacy would be *de trop,* since he practices a superior alternative by the use of his own, inimitable baldertwaddle. I do suggest that while clarity and precision of language may be desirable insofar as obtainable, they cannot be, ought not to be, the sole end of philosophy.

We could have anticipated another one of Marcuse's criticisms of analytic philosophy. By leaving everything as it is, this philosophy fails to undertake, as Marcuse puts it, its "historical task." The criticism is not altogether false, but it will have to be qualified and rephrased before it can be accepted. The point is of interest because it strengthens our grasp of one of the basic defects of Marcuse's thought: his constant oversimplification for the sake of rationalizing his revolutionary objective, and decreeing by ukase what men ought to do without looking at what they have done and why.

Marcuse lays it down that the "intellectual dissolution and even subversion of the given facts is the historical task of philosophy and the philosophic dimension." By "the given facts" I take it that Marcuse means the social facts, the institutional arrangements, the values and mores that make up the philosopher's ambient medium. And by the "philosophic dimension" I take it Marcuse means the capacity or virtue of a philosophy to dissolve and subvert its ambient world. Analytic philosophy not only lacks this "dimension" but boasts that it lacks it: it leaves everything as it is.

Let us first ask, what is the truth of Marcuse's criticism? It is true that the need has at all times existed for the means of

81

criticizing the texture and structure of our lives—our institutions, our values, our categorial schemes, our basic judgments. Today more than ever, I say, because a multitude of social, political, and intellectual factors have eroded the foundations of our morale, the basis of our value judgments.

To the extent that we have no means of criticizing our world, we are beset by evils, some of which may be remediable. By narrowing the task of philosophy solely to the clarification of our ordinary discourse, the new philosophy abandons a job that a good many philosophers, in one way or another, have always undertaken. Since the job must be done, in the absence of philosophers the job is taken on by self-appointed guruvulu, male or quasi-males, all-knowing smart-aleck female journalists and female anthropologists who take quite literally the name of their special competence. "Anthropologists," they assume, know everything about man. Apparently the fact that they live with a few savages for a period of months or years endows them with a wisdom and prudence that is very seldom given to ordinary men in civilized society. One of the many undesirable results of this bland arrogance is that they convert, or rather, reduce, in the dyslogistic sense of the term, difficult and subtle moral problems into facile problems. A society devoid of the responsible means of criticizing itself by competent intellectual techniques becomes at once complacent, confused, and surly. It should be clear that whatever our political or social convictions, our present need for intelligent criticism is greater than it ever was in the history of our civilization. Until not so long ago, the churches were able to guide conduct, and schools and colleges and other agencies were not lacking. And while these agencies were essentially conservative in their "philosophies" they never were, consistently, the apologists for the status quo. The proof of this is to be found in the dynamism of our history, from the days of Jesus, or of Socrates, or the Prophets, or even earlier, to our own day.

Analytic philosophers narrow their task by making a clean-cut distinction between moral philosophy and the acts we perform, which are open to moral judgments. If you ask any one of these new philosophers what, according to his theory, you ought to do, or which is the right or the wrong choice in a given situation, he replies that he cannot, as a professional philosopher, give you any help. If you want advice go to your priest or your psychoanalyst; or ask Edan Wright, Ann Landers, or Margaret Mead. People of this kind can advise you. Philosophers have other fish to fry.

The separation of moral philosophy from "the given facts" is harmful to the whole of our society and to moral philosophy itself. To accept it is to accept uncritically the division of labor imposed on us by the present social arrangements. But is the professionalism with which we are forced to live a desirable state of affairs? By not asking the question the philosophical analysts take it that it is. This process of specialization has been taking place for, perhaps, millennia, and it may be inevitable even in simple societies, not yet dominated by an overpowering technology. But the condition has become considerably more acute among us during the last century—remembering Gertrude Stein's definition of a century as one hundred years more or less. To accept the forced separation of functions as if they were unavoidable or inherent in the life of culture might have been forgivable a few decades ago in a theoretical physicist—until he discovered sin, as Oppenheimer put it, after Hiroshima. It is unforgivable in a man who calls himself "a philosopher." To accept separation supinely is to accept blinkers without protest, in the delusion that one will see and understand the part he looks at better with them than without them. But can a part be satisfactorily understood in separation from the whole?

In fairness to the problem I should point out that in Alasdair MacIntyre's *Marcuse,* the criticism I have reviewed is examined and its validity rejected. I am not convinced, however, that MacIntyre successfully meets Marcuse's attack.

Criticism is not identical with the coarse, wholesale destruction of all of our living arrangements and values. This would not need to be said, did not Marcuse fail to recognize the distinction. A philosophical practice that turns its back on the needs of living men for the sake of an exclusive abstract clarity is morally irresponsible. On the other hand, a philosophical prac-

83

tice that has as its sole *a priori* end the thorough "dissolution" or "subversion," which is to say destruction, of the means of living, is much more irresponsible. It is indeed criminal. Consider: Analytic philosophy leaves everything as it is. It is therefore harmless. And the cost is light. Our society maintains innumerable parasites, it certainly can maintain these harmless, useless scribblers. But Marcuse would blow up everything. Because the drain is plugged, the roof leaks and a few windows are stuck, he would burn down the house. Did one not have it in front of one's eyes, the irresponsibility would be unbelievable.

Unbelievable also would be the granitic quality of our nihilist's mind. In defining the task of philosophy as the intellectual subversion of the given facts and denying it any other aim, Marcuse gives expression to the unbending absolutism of his mind. Such an attitude is thoroughly anti-philosophical. It is not a recent discovery that one of the external marks of a philosophic mind is its willingness to consider contradictory arguments, alternative solutions, in short, to be open and not closed.

We have to ask next how did Marcuse arrive at the conviction that the "intellectual dissolution and even the sub-version of the given facts is the historical task of philosophy and the philosophical dimension"? (*O-D M*, p. 185) Note first in passing that he seems to mean that the task of philosophy throughout history has been one and the same, from the days of Thales to the days of our Heideggerian and Wittgensteinian misery. Note next, and also in passing, that Marcuse does not tell us what "the philosophical dimension" is a dimension of. I shall have to stick therefore to the philosophical task of philosophy and ignore the philosophical dimension. What I ask is, "How did Marcuse arrive at his conception of the historical task of philosophy?" And I take it that by "the historical task of philosophy" he means what philosophy ought to undertake, not what it has undertaken and does undertake, since he does not recognize as legitimate the task the linguistic philosophers undertake.

How did he arrive at his conclusion? He does not argue it; he simply lays it down. Of one thing we can by now be sure, and that is that he did not arrive at it by means of an examination, however hasty, of the goals men have actually sought to reach when they philosophized. Nor did Marcuse undertake a carefully argued analysis of the heterogeneous goals and a carefully argued statement of the reasons he rejected all but that which he laid down. He was as arbitrary, as purely deductive, as regards the historical task of philosophy as he was regarding the function of art. For this reason we must not expect that the examination of his view of the historical task of philosophy will yield a totally new insight into Marcuse's way of thinking. It is, nevertheless, desirable to consider the matter in order to confirm the understanding we already have of his way of thinking by decree, and in order to appreciate the high price he is willing to pay to remain loyal to his nihilistic commitments.

What he seems to have done is to deduce from his nihilistic negativism what the various human tasks ought to undertake. His own single and consistently pursued goal is the wrecking of our society—whether phrased as the dissolving of the given facts or in some other way. Since this is his only goal, everything must serve that goal; other values than the nihilistic have to be ancillary to it or they cannot be permitted at all. But Marcuse is not satisfied with saying, "My goal is the wrecking of the society in which I live." What he says is, "My goal must be yours, and until it is, you are not free, you are a contemptible flunkey of a repressive society." This is the man who would strike our chains from us. Call this way of thinking by any term you have at hand, one thing you cannot claim for it, and that is that it is held with an eye to the historical facts. What he is doing is ramming down our throats his objective or goal. Other thinkers have sought to achieve other goals. But they were wrong. And they were wrong because they did not seek to reach Marcuse's goal.

It is relevant, at this point, to contrast Marcuse's conception of the task of philosophy with the views of two other writers, both men of the Left. I quote first from an interview given by T. W. Adorno to one of the editors of *Der Spiegel,* reported in the September 1969 issue of *Encounter:*

> Philosophy, in so far as it remains philosophy cannot recommend direct steps or changes. It brings about changes in so far as it remains theory . . . Is not theory also a genuine form of practice?

Am I wrong when I interpret this statement to mean that the task of philosophy is and has been the pursuit of truth? Once captured, truth may bring about changes, but it is not its task to bring them about.

The other view of philosophy with which I would contrast Marcuse's conception of the task of philosophy is that of Wright Mills. Evidently Marcuse never talked to Mills about the task of philosophy. Had he, he would have found that Mills wrote his doctor's dissertation on "the sociology of knowledge." In his dissertation he attempted to prove that the task of several eminent American philosophers had been to write apologies for the system instituted by the class to which they belonged. This is not the place to point out the absurdity of the thesis defended by Mills, and much less to explain how, in spite of my sense of the absurdity of the thesis, I found myself obliged to accept the decision of the other members of his committee and to approve the dissertation. But neither Mills' conception of the task of American philosophy, nor Marcuse's absurd oversimplification of the historical task of philosophy is adequate to the complexity and heterogeneity of the facts as we gather them from the history of philosophy.

Consider, first, that the term "philosophy" is as polysemic a term as we have in the language of scholarship or of the market place. Philosophy has meant so many disparate and, sometimes, incompatible activities that it would be impossible within the short compass of a few pages to enumerate even the important ones. I was once advised by a friend who discovered I was worrying about something, "Be a philosopher, don't think about it." But leaving this beauty of this meaning aside (it is less illiterate than it may seem at first sight) the word *philosophy* was once used in learned circles for the activity of alchemists—from whence, as we learn from Jonas' book on gnosticism, we derive the phrase, "the philosopher's stone." The philosopher was a con man who claimed to be able to transmute base metal into gold. And I would not be at all surprised if someone were to prove that these people were themselves the first victims of their own game. But again, leaving aside the obsolete usage, we find that until less than one hundred years ago the term "philosophy" was used as Europeans today use the equivalent in their languages of our term "science"—to refer to knowledge in general, including what we in England and the United States today call "science," the natural and social, or, if you prefer, behavioral sciences. Dalton and Faraday used the term "philosophy" to refer to their activities, and terms like "natural philosophy," "intellectual philosophy," "moral philosophy" were efforts to establish some distinctions within the field of knowledge. But even on our narrowed, contemporary American-English usage of the term, Marcuse's view of the historical task of philosophy can easily be refused by a short canter through the groves of Divine Philosophy and a hurried tour of its Mansions.

To accept Marcuse's defintion is to rule out of the guild a great many thinkers whom we now designate as philosophers. There have been conservative philosophers, reactionary philosophers (whom I take to be quite a different class of persons from the first class), philosophers who sought to achieve a synthesis between different cultural currents, and revolutionary philosophers who sought to dissolve and subvert, at the intellectual level, the systems of which they were part. But there is still more. For whether a man is taken to be a conserver, a reformer, or a wrecker, depends on the standpoint from which his work is viewed, the time the judgment was passed, and other less important factors. Philosophers can be said to have pursued one goal only in the most abstract and not very meaningful sense: in the sense that they look or claim they look for the truth—and a few, I am convinced, actually do. But since Marcuse's "truth" would have been poison to a man like Urban, and Urban's would have been poison to a man like Wittgenstein, and Wittgenstein's truth is poison to Marcuse, to say that these people look for truth is to say very little indeed. But whether philosophers seek for *the* truth or *their* truths, or whether, like Marcuse, they use their philosophizing to rationalize their nihilist objectives, the historical tasks of philosophy —in the plural—have been as many as there have been philosophers worth their salt, and what the task is, or the tasks are, is, first, a strictly empirical question. If after answering the empirical question a man wants to philosophize in his own way, he has a right to say that this is the way he wants to philosophize. But to lay down the law for others is arrogant insolence, overweening cheek. The truth philosophers seek is as varied as their fingerprints, and that goes for the methods they use and the results they achieve. I am speaking, of course, it is hardly necessary to say, of philosophers and not of parrots or men who use philosophy for their own ends.

Although Marcuse knows better, or at least once must have known better—although he showed that he knew better in *Reason and Revolution*—he arrives at the historical task of all philosophy by extending to all philosophers what he has taken the task of his own philosophy to be. His conception ignores the facts.

Before dropping the theme it may not be altogether superfluous to call attention to a fact that the reader must have already noticed, namely that Marcuse is doing exactly what the linguistic philosophers are doing. They have the effrontery to tell us how we should "do" philosophy and how we should not "do" it. But is Marcuse's effrontery any different? With a total disregard of the facts worthy of the logophiliacs, does he not also have the effrontery to tell us what we ought to apply ourselves to if we are to accomplish the historical task of philosophy? Let me iterate that he does to philosophy what he did to art. But his *Diktat* as regards art or philosophy is not an act of scholarship; it is an act of sheer partisanship.

It would be doing a disservice to the reader and injury to the truth were I to convey the impression that *One-Dimensional Man* consists solely of a series of acerbic damnations of the falsehoods by which we live. It is, indeed, as already noted, full of exaggerated virulence that, lacking adequate objective cause, fails to convince a reader who does not initially share the author's unqualified negative attitude. But not all of Marcuse's charges are false. Some are valid, although each one of his readers will want to qualify each of those he can accept according to his own knowledge of our society. And this also holds—let me say it here, although not exactly in place —for statements found in some of the essays published in *Negations.* But *One-Dimensional Man* also contains some opinions that are of interest in themselves, in the sense that all error is of interest to the student of intellectual pathology, and that are also of interest as samples of the perverse extremes to which Marcuse is led by his uncritical negativity.

An accusation against our world with which a large number of his readers—whether to the right, center or left of the socio-political band—will agree is the invasion of privacy from which we suffer. That we can turn off the propaganda, that the attempt to install loudspeakers in railroad stations has so far been defeated, that we do not have to waste our time in front of an idiot box unless we choose to do so, that the invasion of our privacy has not yet reached the damaging degree it reached in China when the gentle agrarian reformers, headed by Mao, took over, that the congestion in our world has not reached the packing it has reached in Japan, that we can still achieve solitude if we truly want it, all of this makes little difference. Marcuse's accusation is not only justified, but what is more rare in the pages of *One-Dimensional Man* it is not couched in acerbic language. The moderate qualification that accompanies the accusation is not usual in his pages. Furthermore, it is written in English, not in Marcusean *papiamento*. He writes:

> Can a society which is incapable of protecting individual privacy even within one's four walls rightfully claim that it respects the individual and that it is a free society? To be sure, a free society is defined by more, and by more fundamental, achievements than private autonomy. And yet the absence of the latter vitiates even the most conspicuous institutions of economic and political freedom—by denying freedom at its hidden roots. Massive socialization begins at home and arrests the development of consciousness and conscience. (*O-D M*, p. 245)

It is only fair to agree that there is some truth in this criticism, but it must be qualified. It can be shown that the development of consciousness in our society is one of its great triumphs, in which we all can take pride. It is to that development that the increase in knowledge, particularly scientific knowledge, and more narrowly still the development in biology and physics that we have witnessed in the last decades, is to be traced. But our consciousness is not confined to the development of pure knowledge; technology has made possible the refinement of our aesthetic awareness. I remember reading over 35 years ago a letter of Thoreau in which he thanked his correspondent for a little music-box the friend had sent him. In what I remember as a genuine expression of gratitude, Thoreau thanks the giver for an instrument that would make his hours more rich. We remember that Thoreau played the flute, and the gift was therefore appropriate. But today a man of little means has all the music of the world throughout the ages of which anything is known easily within his reach, through the phonograph and radio. True, the commercials are a nuisance. But if he can't stand them he can find good records at relatively little cost. And this goes for good reproductions of great pictures and for anything that is food for the spirit.

But a man is not dependent on his income to pursue the good life through the arts. Many agencies are active in lending paintings and records to those who cannot or do not want to buy them. Some of the reproductions are not very good, but they are better than the engravings that were the only possible way of coming into contact with great art in the Nineteenth Century unless one was very rich. By the development of the lending of reproductions and originals by museums and local libraries, the lending of records, production of the classics in cheap paperbacks, easier and cheaper travel, and the enlargement of the scope of instruction in schools and colleges in such a way as to make students at least superficially acquainted with the achievements of our civilization—by these means the depth and breadth of the spiritual life have been increased. Much can be said against these efforts and some of what can be said I have said myself when the occasion arose. But to claim that "massive civilization . . . arrests the development of consciousness" is a charge that Marcuse could not possibly make stick.

And what about the development of the conscience? It is simply an utterly false charge. Indeed, Michael Polanyi in the Thirteenth Arthur Stanley Eddington Memorial Lecture, entitled "Beyond Nihilism," given in Cambridge, England, in 1960, and now available in *Knowing and Being* (Chicago,

1969), made the point, to my mind beyond refutation, that the moral nihilism of our day was not the result of an atrophy of conscience but of the very opposite. One can say that Marcuse himself is a very good instance of this phenomenon. His is an overdevelopment of the conscience that has lost its balance, and is equally outraged by serious defects in our culture as it is by trivial ones, but it is an overdevelopment that grasps neither the serious nor the trivial in perspective and in contrast with other societies. I shall not expatiate on the point in detail. Polanyi's lecture is available. Let me here call attention to the ease with which the New Nihilists can get up a march, a sit-down strike, a riot, for trivial causes that are excuses to wreck our world. And remember how these people behave; remember, especially, their colossal self-righteousness. Their conscience is not underdeveloped. It is overdeveloped and over-developed along lines that could not be more destructive of our values than they are.

It is true—or so it seems to many of us—that massive socialization is not a good but an evil. Noise invades our peace, and we cannot ask our neighbor to turn down his radio or television broadcast when he brings the stupid box out in the yard to hear the game on a hot, humid afternoon. What is more, Big Brother has our number; he has our fingerprints and a big dossier. But consider the freedom we have and that Marcuse would deny us. For all the dope Big Brother has on us, I could still, if I so desired, stand in downtown Chicago and shout, in the late summer of '68, that Old Corn Pone is an unspeakable vulgarian. Nothing would happen to me. A policeman might order me to get going, but I could not suffer prosecution for calling Johnson names, although they might get me to court on a charge of disorderly conduct—quite a different thing from a vacation in Siberia. But imagine what would happen to Ivan Bednyak if he were to stand in front of Lenin's tomb and say the same thing of the ruler or rulers of Russia at the time he chose to speak out? We are slaves, the victims of domination, putty in the hands of a massive civilization that arrests the development of consciousness and conscience but that, when the arrest of consciousness and conscience is defied, shrugs its shoulders and lets us be.

But I need not embroider a point on which I am confident the majority of my readers will agree. Were Marcuse's criticisms always of this nature, were they always followed by the "to be sure" or its equivalent, Marcuse would have today many more admirers than he now has. And these admirers would be endowed with an intellectual sophistication and a moral maturity that I am convinced the majority of his nihilistic followers almost totally lack.

But Marcuse is seldom moderate in his accusations. The upshot is that when on first sight his reader believes that Marcuse has hit the bull's-eye, it turns out on reflection that the validity of his argument is "vitiated" by an abstract generality which is not buttressed by concrete evidence. Take his criticism that we live in a society that arouses desires and needs and wants that do not seem indispensable to the development of our full humanity. *Seem,* for put as a generalization qualified by the "seem" I have no doubt that the majority of us would take Marcuse to be right. But before we can be confident that he is right, we want to examine with care the criterion by which Marcuse arrives at his notion of our full humanity. The theoretical discussion of some aspects of this important question I shall take up below. Here it is enough to point out that it is not likely that we shall agree among ourselves or collectively with Marcuse on those who possess the wisdom to decide on the virtues that make a man fully human and on the vices that diminish his humanity. It takes a very superficial knowledge of what Europeans call "philosophical anthropology," and of contemporary psychology and social science, to know that to get started on this question is to fall into quicksand. Who knows what a fully developed human being is? Plato? Diogenes, the dog? Marcus Aurelius? Paul or Augustine? Hobbes? The Marquis de Sade? John Dewey or Bertrand Russell? The Frenchman with intellectual dandruff on the back of his house-jacket and his paranoid stare of hatred at the United States—Sartre? Or—may *le bon Dieu* save us from our saviors—Margaret Mead or Herbert Marcuse?

This is not to suggest that we must surrender to the facile

relativism that is part of the regnant orthodoxy of our contemporary intellectual climate—a surrender that would soon lead us by a different route, to conclusions as flagitious as those proposed by Marcuse. It is only to suggest that while there is some sort of consensus about some of the disturbing symptoms of disorganization and corruption in our society, and while there is truth and even wisdom in the criticism that we could live a good life without many of the gadgets we are so compulsively driven to load ourselves with, there is no consensus whatever about the concept of man required to make a diagnosis of the etiology of the social malady from which our society is suffering and of its proper treatment. Only a man endowed with the arrogance of a Herbert Marcuse would pretend that he, and only he, has the true knowledge of human nature and can therefore tell us with confidence which of our desires, needs, and wants ought to be aroused and which ought to be discouraged or altogether suppressed.

A second instance of one of Marcuse's observations with which one agrees on the surface is the utterly commonplace fact that we are facing international problems gravid with monstrous calamities. Is there anyone today who would not agree to the truth of the observation? But here again, the general agreement about our difficulties does not lead to consensus about the illnesses or their remedies.

ONE OF MARCUSE'S LAST BOOKS, *Negations,* IS A COLLECTION of essays all but three of which were originally written in German and published in the United States between 1934 and 1938. We also find in it the following items: an essay on Max Weber that was first printed in German in 1964 and was revised a year later, an essay that appears in print for the first time, and Marcuse's review-article of Norman O. Brown's *Love's Body* together with Brown's "reply," both of which pieces appeared for the first time in *Commentary* in 1967.

The first statement to be made about this collection of essays is that their translator, Mr. Jeremy J. Shapiro, has done students of Marcuse and of the society he threatens a very valuable service. To make these essays available to the general American public is to enable us to assess the stature of our nihilist more accurately. Recently a reviewer—it does not matter where the perpetration appeared—dismissed *Negations* with a wave of his hand. But this is an injury to those readers who may accept the reviewer's judgment and miss important aspects of Marcuse's thought.

Not all essays in *Negations* are of equal value to the student of Marcuse's nihilism; but those published in the Thirties are of interest because they show that Marcuse was then concerned with ideas that he was to develop later in his books. These earlier essays, written in German and written to be read, I guess, by his fellow refugees, are considerably more difficult to understand than most of his later work, because to the Marcusean language is added serious concern with technical philosophical analysis and what seem to be passages written in a language shared only by a closed circle of fellow refugees. I shall not give here specific examples of Marcuse's well-known genius for taking any thought, even the simplest, and wrapping it in impenetrable verbiage. I shall take up the problem of his style later. But the reader in search of the germ of some of the atrabilious criticisms found in *One-Dimensional Man* and even some of the ideas basic to *Eros and Civilization,* can find them in these essays. Professor Eric Voegelin told a mutual friend, who passed it on to me, that Marcuse has been saying very much the same thing for as long as Voegelin has known him. Some proof of the truth of the statement is to be found in these older essays. The difference between the earlier essays and the volcanic "defamations" (to borrow another term from Marcuse's vocabulary) of *One-Dimensional Man* is that in the Thirties Marcuse had not yet developed the acerbity that he has been displaying in recent years. But even in the last essay of *Negations,* published for the first time in this book, and we may therefore guess written only recently, "Aggressiveness in Advanced Industrial Society," the tone is milder than that of *One-Dimensional Man.* It seems that during the time Marcuse was writing this essay he had recovered the scholarly attitude displayed in *Reason and Revolution* and in *Soviet Marxism.* The essay reads as if it had been written for sociologists and not for student demonstrators befouling a university president's office. The essay contains plenty of exaggerations and the burning hatred of the defects, real and alleged, big or small, of our world. But the reader does not breathe the atmosphere of *One-Dimensional Man.* It is, therefore, easier to read; easier, however, in one sense only, in that it does not arouse the counter anger easily elicited by uncontrolled hatred.

Two of the essays published in *Negations* furnish us with important material needed to understand *Eros and Civilization* and *One-Dimensional Man:* "The Concept of Essence," and "On Hedonism." The first of these two essays was originally published in 1936 and the second in 1938. Their importance lies in the fact that they furnish part of the theoretical foundations for two books that follow them. For that reason it is necessary to examine their central arguments carefully. However, a satisfactorily exhaustive examination is not possible since it would involve the writing of two essays of at least the length of the two under consideration. I begin with the essay on essence: materialist theory—which is to say, Marcuse's theory—we are told,

> conceives the essence of man as the task of a rational organization of society, to be achieved through practice that alters its present form. Materialist theory thus transcends the given state of fact and moves towards a different potentiality, proceeding from immediate appearance to the essence that appears in it. But here appearance and essence become members of a real antithesis arising from the particular historical structure of the social process of life. The essence of man and of things appears within the structure; what men and things could genuinely be appears in "bad," "perverted" form. At the same time, however, appears the possibility of negating this perversion and realizing in history that which could be. (*N,* p. 67)

What the passage means is that man's essence is not something that he already possesses, or that he possessed in the past and lost. His essence is something to be realized in the future through social action, something that will come to be when we reorganize society rationally. We know what we ought to be by contrast with what we now are—by contrast with the evils and perversions we have suffered from in the past and are still suffering from. Upon "immediate appearance," which is to say, upon the appearance of present evils and perversions, man's essence, which is to say, what he ought to be, appears by contrast. Man's essence, thus, is a potential ideal that we ought to realize. This is, with apologies to Plato, a materialistic platonism, the doctrine of the reality of the realm of ideas and the unreality of worldly things brought down to earth where, as Marcuse would have it, progress from appearance to reality alone can occur. In short, the present, which is evil, is appearance; the future, which is ideal, is reality. (*N*, p. 67) Three pages below the above quotation Marcuse tells us that "in a very general sense, essence is the totality of the social process as it is organized in a particular historical epoch." But this is not to be taken to mean that the essence of man under Hitler and Stalin had been realized in these two systems of tyranny and bestiality, but that in these systems appeared, by contrast, what man ought to be, what man at that time could become, were the systems to be destroyed and society reorganized rationally.

It would be erroneous to interpret Marcuse to mean that he is concerned with the intricate net of specific relationships between man and man in concrete cultural conditions at a given time. Marcuse does not mean that any state of affairs that the future will bring will be the realization of man's essence. The essence is an ideal with which the present is somehow pregnant, to be brought to birth by man's effort. An American-trained thinker would feel compelled to indicate that before the problem of man's essence could be solved one would have to show, first, that man does indeed have an essence, since there are many who deny it, and before proceeding to define man's essence, he would dispose of the problem of the effects of cultural factors on man's essential nature. This is the problem of cultural pluralism and will be discussed below when I turn to the examination of Marcuse's view of true and false needs. Enough here to say that Marcuse's reality is strictly the abstract reality of the Marxist. "Reality, where man's essence is determined, is the totality of the relations of production." (*N*, p. 82) A Marxist, in the habit of thinking in terms like "production," "classes," "historical stages of development," and other such linguistic counters, Marcuse does not stop to think that the relations of production cannot be profitably discussed in general terms, for they vary from factory to factory, from union to union, from industry to industry, from nation to nation.

But Marcuse is not interested in such specific matters, which determine, in part at least, the quality of the life men are able to live. He makes his formal bow to the relations of production and goes on to condemn in general terms the present as bad or perverse, and to hail a vague chiliastic future as perfect. Marcuse also calls attention to the fact that the materialist notion of man's essence, which is to say, Marcuse's notion, is not utopian. He writes:

> These determinations of essence are distinguished from utopia in that theory can demonstrate the concrete roads to their realization and can adduce as evidence those attempts at realization which are already under way. (*N*, p. 73)

But the distinction he draws between utopia and the "determinations of essence" will not do, since the statement assumes that the term "utopia" refers to an impossible state of affairs whereas Marcuse's vision is possible, whether or not already on the way to realization. But the only states of affairs that are impossible, as already noted, are contradictions in terms. All other states of affairs, which he calls "determinations of essence," are possible although few of them are probable. There is no way of showing that Marcuse's or anyone else's notion of the good life in a distant future is impossible; if it is not self-contradictory it is possible. But is it probable? Setting aside the animating passion of our nihilist "philosopher," it is a question between Marcuse's hope and faith on one side, and a prudent and conscientious empiricism on the other. And this again suggests the question: Why should anyone be so imprudent as to wreck his world in the hope of bringing about as remote a probability as Marcuse offers us? Since Marcuse at this time rejected empirical knowledge, and by a process he does not explain—but which we guess is a Marcusean adaptation of phenomenology—he "grasps" the "determinations of essence" in the malfunctioning of our society, there is no objective means of deciding in favor of his fideistic vision and against our hard-won empirical knowledge.

Marcuse wrote the essay on essence in 1936 and although he changed his mind by the time he wrote the last paragraph of *One-Dimensional Man* the foregoing comments on the way he grasps his vision are not irrelevant, for one of the purposes of this study of Marcuse's nihilism is to examine with some care the way our prophet reaches his conclusions and confuses his chiliastic dreams with probable reality.

Let us begin with a passage I have already quoted, and that I shall have to refer to again:

> The critical theory of society possesses no concepts which could bridge the gap between the present and the future; holding no promise and showing no success, it remains negative.

In 1936 the moment had not yet arrived for such hopelessness.

In the essay on essence, Marcuse also suggests that while in the past, for obvious reasons, man could not realize his essence, today he can. He writes:

> At the stage of development that man has presently reached, real potentialities for the fulfillment of human life are at hand in all areas, potentialities which are not realized in the present social structure. (*N,* p. 72)

And he adds, "Here the concept of what could be, of inherent possibilities, acquires a precise meaning." (*Ibid.,* p. 72)

If this means—as I believe it does, for the same idea is expressed at least once again by Marcuse—that our industrial society is already in a position to improve the material conditions of life of every man, woman, and child now living anywhere in the globe, and if it also means—as we have a right to infer from his universalistic ethical hedonism—that because it

101

has the means it has the obligation, I submit that this is nothing but faith. This is discussed by George Kaleb in a recent issue of *Commentary* (January 1970), "The Political Thought of Herbert Marcuse." Kaleb writes:

> The heart of the matter is whether the world could ever have the material basis to sustain the quality of life Marcuse desires.

Kaleb answers in the negative. Were political and economic arrangements "more rational," he writes, "some small progress in alleviation of the poverty and scarcity of the Third World could be made." But it would be at the cost of "the majority of the advanced portions of the world."

Let me note, first, that "ever" is a very small word, but it refers to a very long time. I would substitute for it, "in the foreseeable future." Two other comments are called for: The first is that Kaleb works with the same obsolete notion of reason, as we shall see below, that Marcuse works with. According to this notion, it is more "rational" to feed the less advantaged third of the world than to let it starve. I shall point out that it is indeed more "rational" if one accepts a value premise usually taken for granted today, but which is not self-evident. The second is that Kaleb does not seem to put in question whether the quality of life that Marcuse takes to be desirable is indeed desirable.

What could man become? What "real potentialities" ought we to realize? We have already seen the answer given in *Eros and Civilization:* Resexualized man engages in very little work and less labor, and puts his time into play and display, since technology relieves him from onerous toil. Because the theoretical foundations of Marcuse's ideal of man are expounded in the essays on essence and on hedonism, we must examine them.

WE HERE TURN, THEREFORE, TO THE EXAMINATION OF THE first of these two essays. I begin by noting that Marcuse's doctrine of essence is intimately connected, as we would expect it to be, with the idea of potentiality. But unfortunately he does not throw much light on the latter idea. And this is much to be regretted since his discussion of it would have helped us understand his thought. Although in the absence of explicit indication one cannot be as certain as one would like to be, I shall assume that the term "real potentiality," when applied to man, refers to what man ought to become, and "man's essence" to what he will actually become—once he reorganizes society along Marcuse's utopian plans.

One problem need not detain us. Marcuse's concept of essence is stipulative. But since there is nothing wrong with the stipulation of meaning in philosophical discourse, his usage of the term "essence" need give us no trouble. He seeks to justify his usage by a survey of some of the meanings that have been assigned to the term historically. But this survey is unnecessary in spite of the claim made by Marcuse that his notion is "an advance" on Hegel and Husserl. It is only an advance if the motion is measured by Marcuse's aim, the destruction of our society. But whether the destruction is an advance or a regression we cannot yet tell. It depends on what institutions will take the place of those torn down. For no one but Marcuse's followers will measure the existing imperfections against Marcuse's merely verbal assertion of his hopes. In any case, who are Hegel and Husserl that an "advance" on them should be taken to be an advance towards the truth? In philosophy there is no authority other than the force of the argument.

Although it will involve a slight repetition of what I have already said, it is advisable to begin our examination with a quotation of an important passage from the essay on essence, a few lines of which I have already quoted, for most of my comments will be addressed to the ideas expressed in this passage.

> The critical impulses in the theory of essence, abandoned by eidetics as well as positivism, have been incorporated into materialist theory. Here, however, the concept of essence takes on a new form. This theory conceived concern with the essence of man as the task of a rational organization of society, to be achieved through practice that alters its present form. Materialist theory thus transcends the given state of fact and moves toward a different potentiality, proceeding from immediate appearance to the essence that appears in it. But here appearance and essence become members of a real antithesis arising from the particular historical structure of the social process of life. The essence of man and of things appears within the structure; what men and things could genuinely be appears in "bad," "perverted" form. (*N*, pp. 66-67)

Kindly observe, first, that the passage exhibits once more the fact that Marcuse's thought is consistently controlled by his practical objective and not by the autonomous exigencies of

104

philosophical theory. Indeed, pure theory, as we understand the term, is something in which Marcuse does not seem to have any interest and towards which he manages to convey a rather snide contempt although, unmistakable as the attitude is to anyone who reads with care, it would be impossible to give an example of his attitude in a short quotation. This is what we would expect from a wholehearted activist. To hold a thought, so to speak, at arm's length and behold it dispassionately, to speculate, to contemplate, to theorize, to look on as in the theatre—with which the word "theory" is etymologically connected—is an activity into which Marcuse does not put his time. The non-Marxist takes theory, speculation, to be the polar opposite of action, although he knows well enough the intricate positive and negative connections that exist between thought and action. He knows that theory can originate in the need to satisfy other interests than the exercise of pure curiosity, and that after indulging in the need to theorize for its own sake theory may be made to serve purely practical purposes. He also knows that some branches of inquiry—some branches of the higher mathematics, I am told, and obviously some developments in astronomy—serve no other purpose than the satisfaction of the curiosity of those who are interested in them. Their residential value is enjoyed solely by those who indulge in these activities. Their non-residential values— the values these activities have besides the value of cultivating them for their own sake—are heterogeneous; nor are they always considered to be positive by the coarse pragmatic mind. Other forms of speculation may have their origin solely or chiefly in their utility. We all know the explanation of the origins of plane geometry, and we also know the thesis sociologists of knowledge have defended that the origin of modern physics is to be found in technological demands.

We note next that the concept of man's essence Marcuse discovers in "the given state of fact" is put forth as universally valid without qualification. But those of us who have spent our time observing our fellow men and ourselves, reading history, literature, and philosophy, pondering the problems of philosophical anthropology, and seeking to learn from these efforts what men are like, question the validity of Marcuse's sweeping generalization. Marcuse's concept of man's essence, to be realized in some future socialist state dedicated to the promotion of the play and display of its members, is valid only for Marcusean revolutionists. Non-socialist hedonists take their pleasure where they find it and waste no tears on the misery of the rest of their fellow beings.

We know, also, that revolutionists are seldom hedonists. They tend to be puritans or, worse, they tend to be prudish. Marcuse will reply that they reject his plan for resexualization because they are still suffering from the repression the system they brought down inflicted on them. But has the type of man who caused the two seismic revolutions of our century shown promise of adapting himself to Marcuse's utopian plan? The leaders have discovered something much more intoxicating than polymorphic sexuality; before they wrecked the world they thirsted for power, and after getting it, they found that the exercise of power brings on a vertigo that they had never dreamt was attainable: Blood, *paredones,* corpses, the humiliation of their fellow wreckers, the millions of corpses—this apparently intoxicates the successful revolutionist and deflects, reduces, or sublimates, the erotic drive. The drive of the power maniac is apparently satisfied only with the actual smell of the blood of men—foes or friends turned foes or men standing by trying to remain neutral. Nor is their drive successfully hidden under their pious baldertwaddle about human happiness, with which these maniacs profusely gas their future victims. "The little death" is nothing compared with the ecstatic enjoyment of spilled blood—for these men.

Why doesn't an intelligent man like Marcuse take account, at least in passing, of these considerations? All I can offer in reply is a hypothesis, and I offer it with diffidence. When one becomes familiar with Marcuse's thought, his baffled rage, his arrogance, his intolerance, the contempt that hides under his alleged concern for the victims of repression, his unlimited confidence in the apodictic validity of the vague millenarian dreams and ill-formed yearnings, when after much hesitation one becomes aware of the fact that back of his uncontrolled anathemas, of his fulminations against our world, is to be found a coarse, all-or-nothing, black-or-white manichean intellect, one is suddenly brought up short by something that at first seems impossible, but that the more one turns one's mind to it the more it seems to be the solution of this puzzle. The *mot juste* for this collection of traits is immaturity—moral immaturity. For, if you grant intelligence as I do, how else can you account for the oversimplifications, the boundless confidence in principles plucked out of what seem to be subjective frustrations, the rage at imperfections inflated by the preposterous demands of a chiliastic mind?

We have already seen Marcuse's crude pragmatism operating in his conception of the function of art and the nature of philosophy. It also operates, not only in the formulation of his notion of man's essence, but throughout the rest of his thought. Fundamentally, then, Marcuse is singularly consistent. But whether that consistency, bought at the price of so much exclusion, of so much misinterpretation, of such uncontrolled exaggeration of the facts of contemporary society, aids or obstructs the adequacy (in the scholastic sense of the term) and validity of his thought, is quite a different matter. In some of his works, not all, Marcuse thinks in the way politicians think; he does not think the way the philosopher or the scientist thinks. There is nothing new in the way politicians think. It is probably as old as human society. And it is one of the ways that helped build that edifice of shrewd observation, outraged moral sensibility and partisan mendacity that is the Marxist-Leninist theory.

It is not difficult to see that Marcuse's futuristic notion of essence entails potentialities he believes man is endowed with and ought to realize. But Marcuse has no ordinary notion of potentiality, and the reason for this is that he is no ordinary run-of-the-mill materialist but a dialectical materialist.

If you are a mere materialist, a follower of Democritus and Epicurus or of one of the present-day descendants of these ancient worthies, if you are only a crawling sort of atomistic materialist, and not a hop-scotching dialectical materialist, you have no right whatever to believe that man has an "ontological" purpose or telos, of the kind believed in by Socrates, Plato, by Christians, by philosophical idealists and axiological realists. For a mere materialist things are what they are, and become what they become; and if he wants to know what they can become, he observes their behavior and projects it into the future. To say that a thing has a given potentiality is merely to say that things like it have been observed to develop in a given way. Heavy smokers, it is asserted by some researchers, are potential victims of cancer, and corporation executives are potential victims of stomach ulcers. But the potentiality of a man or thing is not something inherent in it: it depends on the man or thing and on favorable external conditions that can be discovered by observation. If we do not mention them it is because we take them for granted. An acorn is potentially an oak, but only under certain conditions which are known to foresters.

But if you are a dialectical materialist *à la* Marcuse, a turned around, latter-day Hegelian of the Left, the potentiality of man or things is not decided in this manner. How is it decided? The answer that Marcuse gives to this question is not enlightening. For him potentialities are not extrapolations from the past and present to the future. They "appear" in "the given state of fact" as "the essence" to be realized. It does not take much knowledge to know the origin of this armchair way of getting at empirical reality. Marcuse studied in Freiburg, where he was taught to get at essence by a verbally elaborate but substantially simple act of intuition. Anyway, what "appears" is what man ought to be and will be, when he gets resexualized—as I gather from *Eros and Civilization.* We have it then that the essence of man "appears," and that once it "appears" we "grasp" it. It should be noted in passing that to get the essence to appear and to grasp it, apparently, for Marcuse, nothing needs be bracketed. He seems to have simplified the game of essence chasing. But while we may guess what will appear in the given state of fact—resexualized man—he does not tell us anything about the appearance of the essence except that it appears. And this is not enough.

How does it appear? Does it appear as the Angel Moroni

appeared to Joseph Smith? Certainly not. Marcuse is a scarred and bemedaled veteran of many a dialectical materialist campaign, and while dialectical materialists believe that the cosmic process and history move by catastrophic explosions caused by internal contradictions along teleological lines that are not teleological, one thing we may be certain of, and that is that they do not believe in Messengers of the Lord. Then it appears in a dream? Or through the agency of ESP? Or as an image or cadence appears in a poet's mind, enticing him to go on to make a poem out of it?

In none of these ways. One gathers, but one is not quite certain, that the essence makes its appearance by means of, or in or through, an intuition. The hunch is not altogether without ground, since before he introduces his own definition of essence Marcuse speaks a number of times of the intuition of essence, and never detains himself to indicate disapproval of this means of arriving at essence. There are two difficulties with the intuition of essence or of anything else, in philosophy, for in the nonacademic world the word "intuition" is as common as it is vague and useful.

Both difficulties are well known to students of contemporary philosophy. The first is that we run into several meanings of the word in the history of philosophy, and unless the meaning used is very explicitly specified we are left in the dark. Marcuse is not exactly open to this criticism but if his expression, "to grasp," is intended as a synonym for "to intuit," he is open to just as damaging objections as intuitionists are. The second is that the product of an intuition is either certain or it is not. If the former, the intuitionist has to tell us how he disposes of intuitions that are equally certain but contradictory to his own. If the intuitions are said to be corrigible, the act of intuition ceases to play the role that classical intuitionists of diverse varieties have assigned to it, that of giving us true intuitions. Intuition then becomes more or less synonymous with conception, with creative thought, with having hunches or stumbling upon lucky guesses, and what then validates the intuition is the method by means of which it is tested. The problem has been, in short, reduced to that of conceiving and testing ideas or hypotheses or both.

Unfortunately not only are we left in the dark about the way the essence appears in the given state of fact and what it means to say that we grasp it, but we are left utterly in the dark about another problem, and one at least as important as the two we have just sketched: How do we know the essence that appears is the true essence and not a fake one?

Before going any further I should note that I have ignored the "three meanings" discussed by Marcuse, "of the difference between essence and appearance." Attention to these meanings would only burden the exposition unnecessarily, and would in no way modify the criticisms of essence here set down.

I do not believe that the essence of man that appears to Marcuse in the given fact would have appeared to him if he had not read the fact with the lenses of a hedonist and a socialist. What he wants is peace among the nations—which we all would like to have and would get if we did not take its cost to be worse than death. Marcuse also wants freedom from the tyranny of the genital. He wants for others a minimum of labor, whether they want it or not. The fact that freedom from labor is being steadily gained by an increasingly large number of white- and blue-collar workers makes no difference since, as already observed, Marcuse disapproves of the way they use their freedom. Indeed he is willing—as was reported in the *New York Times* some time ago—to assert that the civil rights movement has accomplished nothing so far because the Negroes were choosing middle-class values and he is against allowing them to choose wrongly. The leisure that men have acquired is obviously of no importance since misguided, obstinate men prefer fishing. Although I do not lack sympathy with Doctor Johnson's definition of fishing ("I can only compare [angling] to a stick and a string, with a worm at one end and a fool at the other") I will say again and again that it is an expression of odious despotism for a man to ram his values down someone else's throat. Whether a plain man, enjoying plebeian pleasures, is a lesser man than an erudite nihilist bloated with hatred is a question to which, fortunately, we do not have to turn here.

The theory of essence seems to me inadmissible for the reasons I have tried to give an account of in the preceding pages. The objections already reviewed arose from logical and epistemological defects, as they seem to me, fatal to Marcuse's philosophy. But, still in my view, the most serious objection to Marcuse's futuristic theory of essence is neither logical nor epistemological but moral.

The theory tells us, without so much as a purely formal "I am sorry," that we represent only possibilities that have not yet been actualized and that can only be actualized when Marcuse has his way, wrecks the joint, and proceeds, out of the goodness of his philanthropic heart, to resexualize us. We could become human if we followed Marcuse's advice. But suppose that instead of following his advice, we reproach him for asserting that we are not human now, what do you think he would say? Nothing. For as already noted, animals like ourselves, deformed by "societal" repression and domination, cannot know what they really want, which is to say, what they ought to want. We look like men. But that is the given state of fact. We cannot see, as Marcuse can, what we will be when we become resexualized: how strong, how handsome, how intelligent, how alert, we shall be, how beautiful our women, how joyful and yea-saying all of us will be; what deep peace will reign on earth, what over-brimming contentment will flow from our polymorphically eroticized selves. Slaves cannot conceive true happiness. Only a half-breed, produced by mixing dialectical materialism and Freudianism, can conceive true felicity. But even he can give us no more than a very sketchy idea of this future heaven on earth. And come the day, comrade, you better like it.

But I am confident that many of my readers will agree with me when I lay it down that I am not interested in what man can become in the future if—and kindly note the hypothetical form of the sentence—*if* my future involves the denial of my humanity at this moment in this place. But that is what placing man's essence in the future entails: the denying of man's humanity here and now. Living man *not* a man? To become one when he realizes a vague hope in a

111

distant future the existence of which Marcuse tells us he cannot clearly define today?

Nothing that I have ever done, at work or play, would be worth a damn, not a damn at all, were I to view my life in the light of Marcuse's concept of man's essence.

For this reason I shall not have a splenetic old man, sputtering hatred, tell me that I have not realized my humanity, that I will not be fully human until he wrecks my world and puts in its place rubble and our rotting corpses. Because his notion of the essence of man is—to use another of his favorite words—a "defamation" of our humanity, I find the effrontery with which he denies my humanity insufferable. And you, dear reader, will find the defamation of your humanity no less an insufferable effrontery than I do, if you consider his concept of your essence.

I pointed out above that Marcuse has the right to stipulate how he is going to use the term "essence." But whether he has a right to define its nature in the facile manner in which he does, is a totally different matter. If his procedure seems to you, dear reader, to be philosophically high-handed, all I can say is that the true essence of Marcuse's thought about man's essence has appeared to you in the given fact of his turgid jargon and you have grasped it truly.

MARCUSE HAS ALSO ASSURED US THAT HIS CONCEPT OF
man's essence is not only historical and not ontological, but
that it is not teleological. He further claims that his own materialism goes beyond Husserl's philosophy. I have shown that it
is a peculiar form of crypto-phenomenology, turned upside
down and traveling light. For he claims to "grasp" the essence
of man but dispenses with the bracketing that phenomenology
insists on. Our problem is to find out whether Marcuse's assertions about the non-teleological essence he discovers in the
given fact is indeed what he claims it to be.

An account of man, or of anything else, is teleological if it
posits ends toward which a given process strives that cannot
be adequately accounted for in terms of efficient causes. We do
not say that a machine is a teleological thing, although it is

made to serve an end, since it is man who designs the machine and incorporates the purpose into it when he designs it. Both mechanists and teleologists believe that the component organs of a living organism serve a purpose—reduced to its simplest biological formulation, the purpose of an organism is to maintain itself alive and to reproduce. But the teleologist is not satisfied with a purely mechanistic explanation of an organism. He is convinced that the harmonious interaction of the component organs, addressed to the end of maintaining life and making reproduction possible, can only be adequately accounted for by positing a plan. This plan is logically, but not empirically, prior to the coming to be of the organism; and they say that without the plan the interrelationships of the several functions of the component organs cannot be conceived to work in harmony to the end of the whole. No mere fortuitous coming together of the organs that make up the organism can account for its complex and harmonious functioning. And what is true of the organism as a whole is true of its component organs.

It is not a question, be it noted, of a pull from the future. Rather, it is a question whether the organism obeys a logically prior plan. It is a question of whether the organism was intended to "go" towards the future, or whether it "goes" by an unplanned, a wholly fortuitous concatenation of efficient causes. And this turns into the question as to whether the concept of the whole, of the organism, is logically prior to the growth and interlinkage of the components that enable the organism to achieve its purpose. But logical priority does not necessarily mean historical priority. We see daily how an organism grows in stages, how an acorn, given the external factors that enable it to germinate, grew slowly into the oak it now is. Teleologists believe that a number of factors—component organs and biochemical reactions and purely mechanical processes, fulfill a plan. When the female egg is fertilized by the male, under normal conditions an animal develops in womb or egg and in due time it is born. In our day biology has taken giant strides towards a more and more minute analysis of the processes that are involved in the production of an organism. But whether these intricate processes can be accounted for

114

mechanistically or whether the only way to achieve a satisfactory and exhaustive explanation of their coming to be is to posit a plan, is a question into which the non-specialist has no business barging. But he may be allowed the remark that the popularity among experts of the mechanistic solution seems to the outsider to arise in part at least from a faith and a prejudice that comes to us from the Nineteenth Century. If this is the case, the bitter battle will rage on and it will be long before mankind will see the satisfactory resolution of the conflict.

It is not altogether clear whether, when we turn to men organized in groups, all groups have immanent purposes—purposes inherent in them—other than the most elementary biological ones, and whether, if they have immanent purposes, these were devised by themselves or given to them by an external agency. Men want to survive collectively in their groups, and as individuals; and as individuals they have, until recently, wanted to reproduce and prosper. But what men take prosperity to be differs from group to group and from man to man. For reasons that can be made explicit to a greater or lesser extent, we observe groups pulling together towards goals. But these goals are more or less explicitly self-imposed. And only by falling back on complex metaphysical or theological arguments can we manage to establish to our own satisfaction that all groups and each of the members of a group, have purposes that they must seek to fulfill, other than the elementary purposes of survival and reproduction. But we do not know enough about human associations or about men singly to be confident that we can tell whether or not they are guided by purposes they seek to realize. Of men singly we know that a man's culture gives him his goal even though in his conception of it a modicum of discretionary freedom may enter. But does this hold for all men in all societies? Are there not societies so close to petrified custom that their members accept its goals uncritically? Much more factual information than we now have on this question would be welcomed.

Men often seek to reach their goals and sometimes to go beyond them in a conscious way, driving for what, in terms of their society, is considered excellence. Of human groups we

115

know that their activity has sometimes been carried on with extraordinary energy and other times has been undertaken merely to maintain themselves without unusual exertion. The various activities of human groups differ widely. A horde from Asia sweeps westward, leaving devastation behind it, until it is checked and thrown back. Chalons sur Marne, the name of the plain on which the rush was checked, was burnt into the minds of us men of the West. A desert people sweep west and build a great civilization. We checked them, or rather, Charles hammered them back at Tours, and we glow with pride and gratitude at the recollection. Another, the Mayas, goes into a frenzy of building, and another, the Aztecs, into a collective and overpowering lust for human blood to offer the unquenchable thirst of their gods, as they say. Another conquers and establishes a peace in their domains that relieves all but a few of any singularity—the Incas. Were these enterprises guided by deliberate plans? Only in retrospect can we see the direction of their historical trek. Let us assume there was a plan: Let us assume that the spread of the Aztecs, the Mayas or the Incas, that the spread of the Roman empire, or the British, was carried on by men clear and intent on what they were doing. Still, there would be any number of ways of explaining the movement. Would it be possible to say that as groups they were expressing their potentialities? If we judge by what we know, we would be closer to the facts if we said that groups have an indefinite number of potentialities and that we do not know what makes the group choose this rather than that goal—when they choose a goal.

In respect to individuals the problem is much more complicated, for organized groups differ from one extreme to the other: from assigning to the individual a status and role that are fixed, to letting the individual decide for himself what he wants to be and how he wants to accomplish his aims. Even within the restriction of closed societies, there is still the possibility that an individual will succeed beyond the expectations of his fellows, or that he will merely fulfill more or less minimal expectations, or that he will fail. In an open society like ours no one can predict what a child will turn to, or into.

This is what we know. But we know something else. And that is that no organized group has ever dedicated itself to pleasure exclusively. Individuals have, and classes, and even in cultures that inhibit hedonic enjoyment some men have always found ways of living a life of pleasure. When we speak of Sybaris we speak of a social class in a city, and forget the human sweat and misery that were needed to keep that class in its more or less consistent search for pleasure. I would not say that the population of the world today could not dedicate itself to playing and displaying. Certainly some of the technological tools are at hand to reduce enormously the misery of humanity. And in what Marcuse calls "advanced industrial societies" the reduction of misery in the last hundred years has been enormous. But physical tools alone will not bring about this objective.

The defender of Marcuse will object: "Marcuse never posited man's essence—what man ought to be, the potentiality he ought to realize—by an examination of the past and present; you have yourself noted that this is not the way he does it. Therefore your references to what is and has been are irrelevant." But what then, I ask, is the basis for deciding what man ought to be? Who, besides a crypto-phenomenologist, would today claim that essences appear on the given state of fact? Intuition of this sort—if that is what it is—we can ignore. Outside of such miraculous revelations, we cannot arrive at any knowledge whatever if we are deprived of the little knowledge we already possess. Marcuse is not exempt from the limitations that hold all men down. What he claims to discover in the given fact does not come to him in total ignorance. He brings to the criticism of our society a mind stocked with criteria, desiderata, partial experience (for that is all men can gather) and the limitations inherent in his training and temperament, limitations no man is free from. This is the reason scientists have developed techniques for discovering idiosyncrasies in their thought. If the past and the present are not a basis for deciding what men can be, then neither Marcuse nor anyone else has any more than a purely arbitrary basis for arriving at a decision.

Marcuse's defender will retort that of course we have never

117

known of a group dedicated exclusively to the pursuit of pleasure, but that Marcuse has accounted for this fact satisfactorily.
He points out that until now men have always been the victims
of scarcity, which leads to domination and exploitation.

The argument appears plausible but it does not stand up
when examined. The will to domination, the lust for power
over fellow human beings, often manifests itself independently
of the phenomena of scarcity and plenty and can only be
reduced to these terms by a doctrinaire and a prioristic materialism that brings all human activity down to an often imagined
antagonism between classes. Such an antagonism has existed
and has been the cause of war and destruction. But the facts
do not warrant the reduction of all relations among men to class
conflict. We see the drive to domination over men expressing
itself in small as well as large stages. When you see a teacher
of philosophy—as I have had several unhappy opportunities to
see at first hand—who will use every means in his power to
misshape students into his own image rather than let them
become what they have it in them to be, you ask yourself by
what intricate and ingenious rationalization the drive to lord it
over others can be connected with phenomena of scarcity.

To this we must add the fact that Marcuse has to do some
very fancy ice-skating to rationalize the fact that abundance
brings on a condition that he hates as much as if not more than
the condition of inequality and deprivation that existed before
the development of our affluent society.

Consider hastily another fact. Grant first that in almost all
climates and at almost all times men have suffered from scarcity. There have been nevertheless times when, and places
where, scarcity hardly existed. Hawaiian islanders, before
whalers brought them the benefit of their iron nails and their
venereal diseases, were a people for whom, apparently, plenty
always abounded. While we could not offer them as exemplars
of Marcuse's polymorphic sexuality or Norman O. Brown's
polymorphic perversity, because they lived under the tyranny
of the genital, they certainly were considerably less inhibited
erotically than Americans have been in principle and, until
very recently, in fact. But what kind of lives did these islanders

118

who lived in plenty live? Remember their strangling taboos, their constant warfare, the bitterness and gnawing fear in which, in view of what we know, we can guess they lived; the rivalries and jealousies that must have spoiled their pleasures.

It would not seem, then, as if abundance or deprivation by itself could be exclusively or fundamentally definitive of the quality of the life men live. Extreme deprivation, famine, the ravages of war, no doubt can for a time wreak havoc with the arrangements made by men to live an existence that can be endured and at times enjoyed. But in view of the multitude of factors that work together, and against one another, to account for the quality of the life people live, factors most of which are as yet unknown, dogmatism on this question befits the propagandist, the partisan, the ideologue, not the man trying to understand with humility the puzzling complexities of human existence.

I am not unaware that in *Soviet Marxism,* Marcuse argued that when Marx turned Hegel around, he discarded Hegel's teleology. But I am not convinced by the argument, for what Marx seems to have done was to discard an explicit, unashamed teleology, and substitute for it an implicit crypto-teleology in the form of "historical laws" that have a direction and a goal. But a-teleological laws have no goal, although lawful processes may have a terminal point. There are of course many scholars who seriously believe in historical laws, whether of an a-teleological or of a teleological kind. But what these laws add up to, when you look at them critically, are very vague generalizations constructed to prove that some intuition of which the historian is fond, holds for all history. Look at the historian's intuition carefully and you will see that it is the expression of a faith about how things ought to be based on free-floating, idiosyncratic yearnings and a hope that these yearnings will be realized—if not today, *mañana.* When I hear a physical scientist speaking about a law, Avogadro's or Boyle's or whomever's, I know that back of the formula there are a number of carefully conducted observations, subjected to rigorous tests, deductions and inductions, intuitions and hunches, none of which is allowed to stray from the field of inquiry,

119

definitions that actually refer to states of affairs, in short the complex, not well-defined, but well-practiced procedures that have guided scientific progress from its beginnings—wherever the historian of science may place these beginnings. The conditions that make up successful scientific inquiry—the alleged "scientific method"—are today under discussion. The success of science would seem to indicate that scientists, whatever their formulations of their methods, apply them successfully. But when I hear a philosopher speaking about a law I get suspicious. For long ago I found that when philosophers speak about laws, they are brethren of Solon and Moses rather than of Copernicus and Galileo. Legislators, this is about all these men are: but particularly fatuous ones, since their laws have no sanctions, since they are not backed by the power of a state or group of men organized into a commonwealth, and their sole power seems to reside in the quality of their rhetoric and the force of their unanchored speculations. When they enact laws what they are usually doing is telling us how, in their superior wisdom, the universe ought to be, rather than how it actually is.

A dialectical law has one other defect. When Hegel spoke of the hopscotch of the dialectic, he meant the process to be an ascending one, a going from a lower level to a higher—higher in value. Marx took over the dialectic but did not discard the lower-higher progression. The classless state is higher than the capitalist world, which in turn is higher than the feudal ... and so down to cave man and the presumptuous ape who decided to cross the line. This may not be teleology, but if it is not, then it is the only violation of which I know of Leibniz's principle of the identity of the indiscernibles. Marcuse's failure to decontaminate the Marxist theory of history from all traces of teleology becomes obvious when he tells us in the discussion to which I have been referring, that while for Hegel History is the manifestation of Reason, for Marx

Reason pertains only to the future of classless society as a social organization geared to the free development of human needs and faculties. What is history for Hegel is still pre-history for Marx. (*S M*, p. 2).

I ask, doesn't this statement convey clearly the idea that history moves along definable lines towards a point that can be stated before it has been reached and can be known to be an advance towards a desirable goal? Kindly note that the operative word here is "desirable." What is a process that has fixed goals that can be formulated prior to the reaching of them, that are superior to the point of departure, but that are not generalizations from the past and present, but a teleological process, whether we acknowledge it to be teleological or not?

I conclude that from an examination of the hell of our Affluent Society we cannot gather our potentiality—what we ought to become. Thinkers have arrived at a conception of the end of man by means of metaphysical speculations or by appealing to what they call revelation. But if I am not mistaken Marcuse has no right to say that polymorphic erotic pleasure is the only rational end of man and dismiss all other ends that have been proposed. I suspect the reason he avers this to be man's end is that he is a thorough-paced materialist and a Freudian and, for such a person, what other end could there be for man but the enjoyment of pleasure? The Marxist conceives an end and projects it into the future; a world in which the workers will be the owners and will be free from exploitation. But he stops there. What it will be like to live in the classless state is not specified. The Freudian wants pleasure although Freud did not think man could achieve permanent enjoyment. Give a consistent materialist—dialectical or otherwise—a grounding in Freud and he is bound to choose Eros rather than Thanatos; feed him at the same time the millenarian vision of Marx, and he is bound to conceive of an erotic utopia in which each receives according to his need and each gives according to his capacity.

But what, you may ask me, ought man to become according to you? The question cannot be answered in a sentence or two. It calls first for a theory of man, which is to say for a philosophical anthropology or a philosophy of culture—where the "or" functions as symbol of equivalence and not of disjunction. This is not the occasion to undertake the elucidation of this question.

121

15

MARCUSE'S ESSAY "ON HEDONISM" HAS FOR ITS PURPOSE TO give an account of the distinction between true and false pleasure. The importance of the distinction lies in the fact that the justification for the revolution he would bring about depends on the intolerable condition of the victims of oppression. But the victims do not know their true condition. Marcuse, the Marxist, believes that the victims are mistakenly content with their state, are incapable of discovering what is truly good for them, and are therefore disinclined to do anything to build a good world. At the basis of a radical critique of society there must lie a conception of true and false pleasure that ties the individual's true condition—as distinct from that in which he thinks he finds himself—to the judgment that his life is in truth intolerable. This view, which brings the expert into the revolutionary movement by informing the victims of exploitation of their true state is not Marcuse's contribution. That contribution does not even consist in telling them that they are being cheated by a repressive society. It consists in telling them that they are being deprived of freedom from the tyranny of the genital.

Pleasure, we are told, is true or real when it satisfies vital needs, not only the needs of individuals but those of society. How do we decide which needs are vital? Only Marcuse can decide what you or I vitally need. He may never have met you, may not know whether you like cream in your coffee or take it black. He may not know that you exist. He certainly does not know that I exist, *Gott sei Dank*. But he knows, knows as you and I could never know, what our vital needs are.

There are of course universal needs that are common to all men; but these are organic needs that underlie needs that are the result of "the plague of custom" and "the curiosity of nations." One does not have to know anything beyond the fact that a given animal is human to know that a protracted deprivation of vitamins or iodine impairs his well-being. But Marcuse does not have only biological needs in mind. He has in mind our social, our distinctly human needs. And at this point a serious difficulty arises. For while human needs include biological needs, they also include needs of a "superorganic" nature as to the universality of which we are, and have been for decades, in a quandary. Although dogmatists on both sides of the dispute will not concede it the question is still an open one, for reasons that cannot be gone into here. That man has needs of a merely cultural nature, no one questions. But beyond what appears to be agreement lie radical differences of opinion about problems that must be resolved satisfactorily in order to arrive at an acceptable notion of man's nature.

For instance, thinkers are divided on the question as to whether or not "superorganic" needs can be derived from merely organic ones. Naturalists believe they can be. But no one has yet given us a convincingly detailed account of the point-by-point development of the superorganic from the merely organic. One of the philosophical jobs Freud attempted

123

was his derivation of some of the modes of superorganic experience: morality, religion, art. I have shown elsewhere that he failed in this important task all along the line. Malinowski also attempted it, and wrote a book full of hope, faith and fallacies. Until we resolve this question we are not in a position to utter anything but the most hesitant judgments about man's truly vital needs. Had Malinowski been successful in his derivation no "enlightened" hedonistic dialectical materialist could dismiss men's widespread desire for immortality as superstition. Nor are we in a position to decide in what sense and to what extent any given need is universal. Some seem to be formally universal although materially as distinct from one another as they could possibly be. But the most we can say is that so they "seem" to be. Clyde Kluckhohn was interested in this problem but I am not aware that he did more than pose it. To assume that man has vital needs that require no reference to specific cultural conditions is to ignore the important fact that man, as he is known, has always been man-in-culture. About hominids and that philosophic invention "men before society," we know nothing.

In Chapter 1 of *An Essay on Liberation,* entitled "A Biological Foundation for Socialism?", Marcuse sketches, in a few lines, the biological source of morality. He tells us that,

> Prior to all ethical behavior in accordance with specific social standards, prior to all ideological expression, morality is a "disposition" of the organism, perhaps rooted in the erotic drive to counter aggressiveness, to create and preserve "ever greater unities" of life. (p. 10)

One is grateful for the question-mark in the chapter's title. But the facile disposal of this formidable problem—the problem of the source of morality in the pre-human organism—is hardly worthy of serious attention. Until this problem is solved it is not possible to speak responsibly about men's vital needs. Since Marcuse has not solved the problem we can conclude that he has not avoided the vulgar Marxist error of considering human beings as if they were solely the products of the economic

124

determinants of social groups, in abstraction from all other specific cultural factors. With the categorial scheme of oppressor and oppressed, to which Marcuse adds that of true and false needs *in vacuo,* he has an easy time solving problems that have not yet been solved. He tells us what he means by false needs:

> "False" are those [needs] which are superimposed upon the individual by particular social interests in his repression: the needs which perpetuate toil, aggressiveness, misery, and injustice . . . Most of the prevailing needs to relax, to have fun, to behave and consume in accordance with the advertisements, to love and hate what others love and hate, belong to this category of false needs. (*O-D M,* p. 5)

He goes on to say—and I am following the text here quite closely—that the prevalence of repressive needs is an accomplished fact and that repression must be done away with in the interests of the happy individual as well as in the interests of all those whose misery is the price of our satisfaction. He adds that "the only needs that have an unqualified claim for satisfaction are the vital ones—nourishment, clothing, lodging at the attainable level of culture." (*Loc. cit.*) Further on, in the next page, Marcuse tells us that,

> In the last analysis, the question of what are true and false needs must be answered by the individuals themselves, but only in the last analysis; that is, if and when they are free to give their own answer.

This sounds like Lenin's gag about the workers not knowing their true interests and therefore needing the leadership of the Bolshies to tell them that what they really needed and wanted was to substitute the relatively milder despotism of the Czar for the total and naked control of Lenin's thugs of the Cheka.

Let us ask: Do we know any more clearly now than we did before what distinguishes true needs and wants from false ones? Not really. Marcuse tells us that true needs cannot be satisfied in our society. And we know that at least some of the

125

needs he considers true are those he discusses in *Eros and Civilization*. But further he does not go and one naturally wonders if those he is concerned to discuss are meant to be the substance of human life in his "rational" society.

It was at the time I was pondering the problem of the lack of concrete details about the values that will make life happy in his rational world that I came upon another trait of Marcuse's thought that at first I found difficult to believe was part of his way of thinking. The whole discussion of pleasure, happiness, and true and false needs, is carried on by Marcuse in a thoroughly abstract manner. He is not interested in the specific substantive satisfactions and frustrations men meet in daily life or will meet in his dystopia. His thought is above such details. Therefore they do not affect his criticism of our world. The instances he gives of what our hellish society makes us want are, many of them, obviously trivial. Because he speaks in an outraged manner of these things, one does not raise the question about the nature of his thinking. One assumes uncritically that he thinks empirically. He is rejecting an actually existing society, and therefore one believes that he has actualities in mind. His target seems to be concrete. Is it?

We have before us two problems. One is the examination of his discussion of our vital or real needs. The other is the method he employs to arrive at his conclusions. In the following pages I discuss the first of these problems. Later, after finishing the examination of the substance of his thought, I turn to the methodological problem.

What I want to show is that Marcuse's discussion of needs and drives is speciously concrete, in total disregard of the way in which a culture informs values and shapes needs and interests. He thinks of man under repression at present, and reëroticized in the future, as if his real needs and wants arose in the same way everywhere. He sees man today suffering in the hell of our Affluent Society, and in the future playing and displaying. But at the basis of his radical criticism of the present lies an unexamined assumption, namely the belief that all men in a given historical period are alike and need and want, or on "rational" grounds can be made to need and want, the same

126

things. The factor of cultural pluralism and the difficult problems it brings in its train do not interfere with his thought. By ignoring these problems he is able to make directly for his goal. He does not have to distract himself by theoretical obstacles that would considerably delay him, if they did not prevent him from reaching it altogether, were he to notice that they are relevant to the adequate resolution of his basic question: How can one tell true from false needs and wants?

Before proceeding let me emphasize that I am using my terms with care. I mean cultural pluralism and not cultural relativism. Marcuse's thought is carried on, levitated high above the concrete facts of cultural experience. He makes a large number of references to the specific gadgets the members of our society want. But this does not bring him down to cultural reality. It is necessary to go into this matter at length: the majority of our needs and wants seem to be, in Krober's term, superorganic. They seem to arise somehow from culture itself and do not seem to have, or have not yet been shown in detail to have, a traceable connection with somatic processes considered in abstraction from culture. I place emphasis on the term "seem," because usually the hypothesis is taken to be established by appealing to a mysterious process called "emergence." This is obviously an explanation of the obscure by the more obscure.

That culture is rooted in biology is therefore a hypothesis. It is endorsed by the magnificent scientific triumphs of the last hundred years, and the climate of opinion that these triumphs have created. It is psychologically irresistible, and a man has to be totally disregardful of the opinion of the majority of the experts to declare it to be false. But it is a hypothesis for which no proof has yet been adduced, of the kind adduced by, say, Darwin for his hypothesis. It is hardly necessary to say that the endorsement of a climate of opinion is no proof. Taken as a fact — as it is usually taken—the hypothesis begs for naturalism the very problems it should be putting its energy into solving. In any case, whatever connections cultural forms will be found to have with biological processes, the different value patterns found in culture indicate the need for taking culture into con-

127

sideration when we discuss needs and wants. It is true—as noted—that we have tried to go beyond the atomistic consideration of cultures to the more or less reluctant realization that there are cultural universals functioning in cultures. We also accept the view that cultures must be grasped as wholes if we are to understand them and their components, and the modal personality types they favor. But the idea of cultural universals is far from satisfactory when conceived, as they seem to be conceived today by thinkers, in nominalistic terms.

In *Negations* Marcuse tells us any number of times that the wants and needs he is thinking about are actual and possible needs and wants, realized or to be realized, but in history. It is of the utmost importance for his theory to assert that the problem is an historical one. But I have already noted that this is as far as he goes in anchoring his discussion in cultural reality. Remaining general, the reference to "history" is not enough to define specific needs and wants, particularly when we remember that in "The Concept of Essence" he tells us, "Reality, where man's essence is determined, is the totality of the relations of production." (*N,* p. 82) This leaves out much too much from man's essence. To place needs and wants in history, ignoring cultural factors other than those of production, is to fail to see how needs and wants that from a biological standpoint may seem to be artificial and dispensable, from the cultural— not merely from the historico-economic but, from the concrete cultural—standpoint have their own kind of reality, urgency and indispensability. But for Marcuse there are only true and false needs and wants claimed to be historical, but arising *in* cultural *vacuo.* The true needs and wants, he promises vaguely, will be developed in freedom someday when he manages to make us regress to the polymorphous erotic state of the infant. The false needs are those developed by the agencies of repression that keep us in bondage. They will wither away, no doubt, in Marcuse's dystopia.

Let us take a concrete case, to sharpen the issue. The present-day Lacandones, lineal descendants, it would seem, of the Mayas, know nothing of the needs and wants of their glorious ancestors who observed the heavens with—it is said—incredible accuracy, in spite of the crude instruments they had, and who built magnificent temples and developed what in many respects was a high civilization. Nor do their descendants, who have slid back to a primitive state, know anything of the need Marcuse and our academic colleagues have for using our minds in the elucidation of theoretical puzzles. But on Marcuse's theory—he would not draw the inference, of course—neither his needs nor those of our colleagues, nor the needs of the ancestors of the Lacandones, are true needs. And the reason is that Marcuse's needs and the needs of our colleagues and those of the Mayas in the days of their greatness, were needs and wants that have arisen and flourished in repression and not in freedom.

I would grant without reservation that repression can affect needs. But it would be wrong to allow that it puts in question all needs that arise within it. I would insist that the question whether a need is false or not is a casuistic question, to answer which Marcuse has not given us the theoretical principles. Further, in this connection, it is very important to notice that in his discussion of our false needs and wants Marcuse refers only to the household tools that save work and some superficial fads, perpetrations of Detroit and Madison Avenue.

Let me dwell on the point that the vital needs he mentions in *One-Dimensional Man*, "nourishment, clothing and lodging at the attainable level of culture," (5) are a stingy list of true needs and wants. The fulfilling of them, alone, could not make a satisfactory life at the attainable level of culture to which, with our material and spiritual resources, we can rise today. For all his occasional references to culture in the honorific sense of the term, and his acknowledgement of "spiritual" needs—an acknowledgement that he makes only a very few times within the range of my reading of his work—one gets the idea from his pages that beyond physically fondling one another (in a state of freedom from the tyranny of the genital), listening to the music Marcuse likes, drinking the wines he approves of, talking about the topics that please him, reading Brecht and Beckett, and hating what he hates, what we may expect from his dystopia is a mean, narrow, stingy and tarnished existence.

In Marcuse's dystopia a large number of values will be missing, and few of the great figures of history would be allowed to flourish. Audacity, daring, adventuresomeness, courage beyond the call of duty, that dash of deviltry that adds piquancy to dull living, deep passion, and a sense of piety towards our ancestors who built a civilization which produces such diverse types, including the Marcuses—all this will be unknown. The hair-shirt would be a sign of a man or a group's profound perversion, and men like Armstrong, Aldrin, and Collins would be held in contempt and sent to Siberia lest their madness infect their fellow citizens. Not once do we find in his pages a faint expression of his sense of what we owe the past, the great inheritance of which we are such undeserving heirs, or even a slight suspicion that without that inheritance our life would be inconceivably poorer and shallower—the sense, in short, to which Paul Elmer More, whose words I am loosely paraphrasing, gave expression.

That the components of the good life permitted us by Marcuse are indeed essential to the good life, I do not want to put in question. Of course they are. Man cannot live well in a cave or in a tepee. Running water and working sewers are essential to cities, and cities produce thought and art that purely agricultural societies do not seem to produce. But for many men, men of intelligence and sensibility, the vital needs allowed by Marcuse do not at all represent all the needs the fulfillment of which would enable them to say that they are living a good life.

Between ourselves and the Xetás, living in the inaccessible interior of Brazil, there is no difference whatever in humanity. We owe them as much respect as we owe one another. But between their lives and ours there is a distance that cannot be measured. Marcuse's stingy and embittered "Reason" functioning in a cultural *vacuo,* seems to know very little of these differences. It takes it upon itself to define our true needs and to declare that most of our needs are false. And that, for Marcuse's Reason, is the end of the matter.

That cultural needs specific to a group must be met in order to keep the culture going, even when they are radically repug-

130

nant to members of other cultures—this is old knowledge. Therefore I do not need to go any further into it. What is called for at this juncture is to bring up the point in general terms, connecting it, still in general terms, with the difficult tangle of problems regarding cultural pluralism, in order to show that Marcuse's rationalistic, aprioristic, purely speculative approach to the problem of needs and wants is unacceptable. It is unacceptable, not only because Marcuse fails to take account of the heterogeneity of needs we discover among men in different cultures, but also because he seems to assume that all he need do is to declare a need irrational for it to become a candidate for elimination. The matter is not quite as simple, as a man who knows Freud ought to know. The Queen of Hearts can order heads off, but wise statesmen, legislators, reformers, and even despotic revolutionists live in the world of actuality, a world that refuses to be totally yielding to the "rationalist's" fancy. Needs can be uprooted, but to what extent and at what price is a strictly empirical question. The result of elimination is often catastrophic. Marcuse, however, having decided theoretically that a need is irrational, fails to consider that what from an abstract, unempirical point of view may be taken as an undesirable custom often plays a fundamental role in making the life of the members of a given culture possible and significant.

This is to say that Marcuse lacks altogether the sense one can acquire by going to school to American anthropology. Today, one can lay it down flatly that the job of defining true and false needs cannot be taken on unless one has spent a good many hours with the reports we get from field work. True, like men or boys who go to school—any school—the man who goes to school to American anthropology will encounter much nonsense, and particularly on the question of needs and wants. For the majority of anthropologists take these to be culturally determined, without further qualification. But if the student is careful he need not be infected by the relativist germ. In any case he will come to realize that the heterogeneity or pluralism of cultures cannot be left out of account in the consideration of human needs and wants. It need not be stated explicitly that what I have been skirting is the question of the definition of

131

man. For the dogmatist—whether theological or revolutionary —the matter presents no difficulty. To the irenic mind the problem is, to put it minimally, formidable.

If we are honestly concerned with men's needs, and through their satisfaction with men's happiness, the questions I have sketched cannot be answered in general terms; given the heterogeneity of needs and the diversity of their hierarchical arrangements they raise casuistic questions. Some needs are infrangible and ineradicable, but no general criterion will tell us which are and which are not, in a given culture. We know that the impossibility of fulfilling cultural needs, or of repressing these needs—for whatever reason—may bring about devastating consequences to individuals and cultures. But not all intrusions are equally fatal. Primitive tribes have been destroyed and flourishing nations demoralized by change, others refused change, and others assimilated it with ease. Spaniards have shown a capacity to hang on to their traditional ways that may seem tragic or heroic, depending on the point of view, but that shows them to be culturally tenacious creatures. The Japanese have successfully borrowed Western ways and knowledge but their nature, it is said, remains essentially untouched. All of this is stated tentatively, for I may be wrong about the instances I have put down. If I am, I am confident that other examples that are true could be found. And this is stated with diffidence since, in the absence of solid knowledge on this matter, I cannot allow myself the luxury of dogmatism. It cannot be reiterated often enough that on this question, as in so many others, dogmatism is the expression of a despotic, not of a questing mind. We must object to Marcuse's discussion of vital and false needs because it is carried on with dogmatic *hubris,* in an intellectually intransigent manner, and with indifference to stubborn social realities.

Since we cannot in the abstract decide on *a priori* grounds the genuine or spurious nature of a given need, we are forced to guess, to try tentatively, and to wait and look for the results of what happens when a need is allowed to fulfill itself or is summarily denied. Take only one instance. So far as my limited information goes, it is only very recently that scientists have become aware of the problems that the density of population and the lack of elbow-room give rise to. They seem to have found out that overcrowding is deleterious to physical and moral health. This might have been guessed. But guessing is not knowing. And they also seem to have found out that different peoples have different needs for elbow-room. At the moment no other decision about these matters is possible but the purely tentative, solely speculative one. Rationalistic definitions, *a priori* decisions as to what is vital and what is false, are more closely related to the caricature of medieval philosophy I heard about from a pragmatist, as a graduate student in Wisconsin, than they are to acceptable thinking. A pragmatist preacher, well known for his atheistic and relativistic sermons, his sentimentalism and his shallowness, used to tell his classes that when a medieval schoolman wanted to know how many teeth a horse had he consulted Aristotle.

Let us note that the treatment of needs *in vacuo,* given us by Marcuse, is not only theoretically defective, but can sometimes have catastrophic practical consequences for the man who tries to act on it. This can be shown by a recent example. The chief piece of equipment that Ernesto Guevara took to Bolivia with him was his Marxist way of looking at society. For him it was only a question of distinguishing the oppressed Indians from their oppressors. A very easy problem, particularly in South America where only a blind man could fail to distinguish "la gente del pueblo" from "la gente decente": the lower from the upper classes—the Spanish terms I have just used were current in Venezuela when I was a child; I am aware that they carry in them an odious valuation which I do not espouse. The city communists were expected to help Guevara with his "war of liberation." Knowing the nature of communists he knew he could count on that. But the comrades in the cities did not turn out to be what theory led him to expect. And the Bolivian Indian is not merely an exploited human being. Suffering from malnutrition, feeding on potatoes cultivated by primitive techniques employed by his ancestors before Pizarro, living close to the level of the brutes that surround him, ill-used, apathetic, chewing coca to keep going, under the

133

heel of arrogant patricians, in theory he looked like dry tinder ready for the match. Guevara seemingly did not stop to consider that this burdened creature kept himself going by traditional habits and ingrained attitudes that could not be reached by the fancy *taki-taki* of the Marxist. It is not impossible that he could be aroused to "act" against those who misuse him. But he was not aroused by the kind of appeal that Guevara made to him. And the pragmatic test of my assertion has already been recorded by contemporary journalism. Thank Heaven, Guevara's failure was total. I am not saying that I am glad the poor Indian continues under the heel of his exploiters. I am saying that I am glad Guevara failed to start, in South America, one Vietnam, two Vietnams, three . . .

The abstract treatment of man frees one from the irksome chore of referring to specific times and places. A man has a much better, more efficient, comfortable and certain way of reaching his conclusions. So did the schoolmen who refused to look through Galileo's tube. What are his means? He defines true needs conceptually as vital needs, as we have seen. But what does "vital" mean? The term does not have reference to the morale of a people or the strong needs and desires felt by individuals, which is to say felt by men who accept the specific conditions of their survival as the individuals they are, and work within these conditions, and not as the a-cultural men and women that Marcuse takes them to be. But if the term does not mean this, what can it mean? "Vital" means whatever is essential to the establishment and maintenance in some distant future of a vague socialistic hedonic dystopia.

Let me dwell on this theme a little longer. That there are vital and false needs is of course granted. But granting the distinction is the beginning, not the end, of the problem, which immediately becomes inextricably complex or nearly so when we remember that even biological needs are informed by culture. Food is an obvious instance, since groups do not find all nourishing stuff acceptable. Gandhi is reported to have said that India without its cows was inconceivable. But it is also said that while victims of starvation lie in the streets unburied, the cows do not die of hunger. And a good Egyptian, as

134

Herodotus reports, would die of hunger rather than eat pork. Not only are foods subject to cultural selection but sexual practices and even the elementary processes of elimination are subject to the formative forces of culture. Thus it seems that even those needs that could be called distinctly organic and are most elemental are not utterly free from cultural in-formation. Remember King Lear's answer to his daughters, when they questioned his need for the hundred knights.

GONERIL.   Hear me, my lord.
                 What need you five and twenty, ten or five
                 To follow in a house where twice as many
                 Have a command to tend you?
REGAN.   What need one?
LEAR.   O, reason not the need! Our barest beggars
                 Are in the poorest things superfluous.

But since the need must be reasoned, in spite of Lear's magnificent retort, to reason it properly we must come to the job with different standards and an attitude totally different from that which Marcuse brings to the judgment of our needs. First, more tolerance. The despotic attitude is unbearable. Why should he want to turn every man, woman, and child into a polymorphous and narcissistic erotophiliac? His goal is unintelligible as well as unacceptable. We have enough of tyranny, insane despotism and bestial criminality, enough of brown and black shirts, enough of red banners and red and black armbands. Second, a more catholic attitude towards man. Marcuse is a curious paradox: a kind of latter-day jansenist or puritan in small case and a hedonist. Play and display. The whole thing would be comical did we not still have in our nostrils, as Bellow put it somewhere, the persistent redolence of the chimneys of Belsen and Auschwitz. Next, the intellectual humility to listen receptively with the third ear, in order to discover the whys and hows of man's millennial insanity. One cannot trust the intellectual *hubris* of a man who has found the key to the millennial problems and has contempt for us because we are not easily convinced. When one asks him what is the key he

135

answers positively, "Scarcity and domination." In its vacuous simplicity it is not very different from a man who will tell you, with the conviction of a zealot, that what is wrong with the nation is the Communist Conspiracy. Communism is still a danger, for the Reds have not given up the idea of conquering the earth. But it is not the sole danger.

The problem is not merely that of scarcity and domination—these factors cannot be minimized in importance. But it is also a problem containing other factors, one of which is as yet obscure, and one that Marcuse with his Eighteenth-Century rationalism and in spite of his psychoanalytic knowledge cannot even glimpse: the problem of deliberate although unconscious self-deprivation. Could this self-deprivation be the answer of man's mind to the urge for satisfying needs that have little to do with hedonism as usually understood? We can hardly formulate the question in a clear way, but we sense there is a question here that needs be asked. Could this self-deprivation be connected with the fact that hedonism—as a philosophy of life, as contrasted with hedonism as the ethos of a people—only begins to inundate a society when its dikes have begun to leak and threaten to break down? When faith has lost its force—whatever sustaining faith, for history shows that the faiths that have sustained man in his course have been diverse—what can men fall back on to enable them to carry on? In the train on the way to London Rupert asks Gerald, in *Women in Love,* what makes his life center. Gerald has no answer, but Rupert says that for him it is woman, "seeing there is no God." The answer was already old when Rupert gave it to Gerald. Matthew Arnold, hearing the sea at Dover Beach fling the eternal note of sadness, saw that

The Sea of Faith
Was once, too, at the full, and round earth's shore
Lay like the folds of a bright girdle furl'd
But now I only hear
Its melancholy, long, withdrawing roar . . .

We know how Arnold thought the threat could be met, when he found himself on a darkling plain swept with confused alarms of struggle and flight. "Ah, love, let us be true to one another!" There is very little in common between Arnold's request for mutual fidelity as a solution of his problem and Rupert's search for a woman who would solve his. But there is enough in common for us to see that faced with a somewhat similar predicament they seek for a solution in a somewhat similar province of experience.

When a person or a people loses its faith almost any goal will do, for life becomes too heavy a burden to carry on without one. But will pleasure do for a goal? It does not seem likely but a dogmatic answer, either way, is unwarranted.

Marcuse does not agree with this doubt. All our guiding values are false; abstract "Reason" points to nothing but the pleasure that the animal is capable of. All else is sham, when it is not gratuitous cruelty and iniquity. While the body remains capable of the enjoyment pleasure is a good, indeed it is the only good. When it is not, for such unfortunates the "truth" of life reveals itself without cosmetics on its nauseating face. The big and the little hypocrisies that keep life from going berserk don't work. Like the chair of a trainer in a cage of big cats over which he has lost control, the common decencies are useless. The snarling cats tear at one another and threaten him. In the midst of rampant hatred there is nothing for men to hope for but pleasure; that alone is real. It is only chance that brings a man into the world in Germany or in the United States. And if by the same chance a man is a member of a persecuted minority that happens to fall into the hands of a monster, how can we expect him, one of the victims that gained safety, to display any piety towards any group? We know that even his own people may become hateful to a victim of iniquity. We have seen members of persecuted minorities sometimes show hate towards one another. For such a victim all groups are evil, and the realization that this one is monstrous is transcended by the realization that this one shows the monstrous essence of all groups that have ever been. For such a man there is only one

137

straw to grasp at: his dream of a future that will be perfect, and for him there can be only one value that is real, and that is this moment of pleasure and the hope of the next.

But the thinker, it would seem, is committed to another value, the value of truth. Is he? What is truth? He has seen its power—in combat. He cannot be, he will not be, fooled. Marcuse tells us that

> truth is a value in the strict sense inasmuch as it serves the protection and amelioration of life, as a guide in man's struggle with nature and with himself, with his own weakness and his own destructiveness. (*N,* p. 266)

Holding this crassly pragmatic notion of truth, it is no wonder that he is blind to one of the supreme glories of our civilization: the enormous advances, in both a relative and an absolute sense, that it has made in pure knowledge.

I BELIEVE THAT WE ARE ENTITLED TO CONCLUDE, AT THE
very beginning of our discussion of Marcuse's essay "On Hedonism," that his views are—to use one of his favorite words—
vitiated by his simplistic way of conceiving men in a cultural
vacuum. But crippling as it is, this is not the only defect to be
found in Marcuse's essay "On Hedonism." His discussion also
fails to make the indispensable distinction between psychological and ethical hedonism. The failure forces his discriminating
reader to make decisions about Marcuse's meaning that Marcuse should have made for the reader.

Psychological hedonism is the doctrine that whatever we do
is ultimately done in order to obtain pleasure or avoid pain or
both. We may not always know it, we may often believe that
we are acting on the loftiest motives and at the price of severe

sacrifice. But in the last analysis it is pleasure we seek; there can be no other goal. Or rather, there can be another, if one posits Freud's death instinct, which Marcuse takes seriously but excludes from his view of the future. On the other hand, ethical hedonism argues that the only motive for action ought to be pleasure and the avoidance of pain. The presence of the word "ought" in the statement and its absence in the case of psychological hedonism makes the difference between them. In contemporary philosophical lingo ethical hedonism asserts either that pleasure is the only value or that it has the primacy over all other values.

Psychological hedonism is grounded in the rationalistic assumption that comes to our contemporary world through Descartes from as early a source as Plato and Aristotle. The assumption is that of the unity of the human mind. We can make valid generalizations about men because in some essential sense men are all alike, or possess the same faculty: below the profound psychological and institutional differences we display lies the same kind of mind. Only when we make this assumption can we believe that all motivation in all men can be reduced to the search for pleasure—or to any other single motive, for that matter. If the assumption can be challenged, a general law based upon it must be suspended until the assumption is established. But the belief in the unity of the human mind is not a universally acknowledged proposition. Taken for granted in the Eighteenth Century, in the Twentieth large numbers of social scientists, students of philosophy, and the generally "educated" public have denied its validity. The reason for the denial is to be found in the debates, still continuing, on the problem of cultural relativism. I have attempted to demonstrate in writing that this tenet of the dominant liberal orthodoxy is a nest of fallacies and confusions. But the point is, not that cultural relativism is right or wrong, but that we cannot any longer posit the unity of the human mind as if it were self-evident or a question as easily proved as, say, Hume thought that it was. Marcuse fails utterly to notice the problem. And in so doing he begs a difficult and most important issue. For until he shows that men everywhere, irrespective of the

140

cultural factors that differentiate them, have equal needs, he cannot generalize for all men regarding true and false needs. We arrived at the same conclusion above by a different route.

But even if his unproved assumption regarding the unity of the mind of man did not militate against Marcuse's psychological hedonism, his failure to notice the difficulties entailed by tying hedonism to a drive psychology makes his theory of man totally inadmissible. In the essay under discussion, Marcuse makes a point long known to students of moral philosophy. He puts it in this way: "It is true, of course, that men intend not happiness but, in each case, specific ends whose fulfillment then brings happiness." (*N,* p. 196) Thus Marcuse brings up, and in two lines solves the complex question of the relation of drive psychology—or intentions, in this quotation—and pleasure and happiness. Had he analyzed the statement with the thoroughness it demands he would not be open to the charge that his view of man is false in fact and simplistic in logic.

Let us consider drives. They are the psychological springs that impel or push men towards that which they would have. Drives make for their "objects," which is to say for that which does away with the repletion or depletion that appears in consciousness as the drive. Upon reaching its goal the drive disappears altogether or ceases to produce sufficient tension to create discomfort. When the drive achieves its goal, or attains its object, pleasure is experienced as a by-product—usually, but not always. When the drive has been satisfied, perhaps only once or maybe several times, the reappearance of the drive leads not only to efforts to obtain its object but also to the expectation of pleasure.

Since this matter is central to the theory of psychological hedonism and is one on which a great deal of confusion reigns, it is desirable to state the argument from a slightly shifted standpoint. It is simply false to assert that drives seek pleasure *tout court.* There is no doubt a drive to pleasure—although it seems to vary widely from person to person and arguments have been offered that it varies according to somatotypes. But grant that there is a drive to pleasure. And grant further that there are psychological hedonists who seem to be moved by

141

little else than the desire for pleasure; "seem to be," "by little else"—for whether a man can be a consistent psychological hedonist is in theory denied by the examination of the nature of the drives I am undertaking, and would in the last analysis be an empirical question. In any case, specific drives, properly speaking, seek satisfaction through their proper objects, and the more so the stronger the drives are. If it were possible to elicit pleasure or reduce pain or discomfort without the satisfaction of the drive—and this seems today to be the case by the manipulation of the brains of animals through electric charges —the result of the lack of satisfaction would be the same as if no pleasure had been elicited. This holds for the satisfaction of a drive whether the drive seeks the repletion or the discharge of an organ. Thus in the Matto Grosso there grows a palm tree the heart of whose trunk is capable of killing the pain of hunger without nourishing the eater. Men eat it. But the hungry man's need for food is not thus done away with and he will finally die if all he finds to eat is this palm. To say, as psychological hedonists say, that men act for the sake of pleasure, is simply to accept a coarse hypothesis which ignores essential distinctions. At the descriptive level, we can say that men act both for the sake of fulfilling their drives and for the sake of the pleasure the fulfilling provides. But if pleasure were the objective of action, the baby would die of hunger before he had his first meal, for prior to the first feeding he knows no pleasure, unless we posit an innate knowledge of the pleasure to be anticipated from the first feeding—an *ad hoc* patching of the theory that begs the problem. When the exclusive choice of either pleasure or the fulfilling of a life-preserving drive is forced on one, the latter takes precedence. Of course, a gourmet does not eat for the sake of food: he is a hedonist in this respect. And neither did Don Giovanni, perhaps, conquer women out of a starved satyr's irresistible drive. His need was probably not physical; it probably had its source, as D. H. Lawrence would have put it, in "his head."

But even these statements, closer to the complexity of the phenomenon of pleasure as they are than Marcuse's simplistic hedonism, do not do the phenomenon justice. Thus, given the

142

ethos of our society, for a large number of our population, probably, sexual intercourse is indulged in solely for the sake of pleasure. But there must be somewhere religious or physically handicapped men who indulge in sexual intercourse only from a sense of duty. For these men the sexual act could well be unpleasant. Louis XV may have been in the latter class. I need not go into further details on this point. There are idiosyncrasies about the capacity to enjoy pleasure that would prohibit a cautious thinker from generalizing, from painting, as is said in Spanish *con brocha gorda,* with a fat brush.

It is far from being the case that the fulfillment of drives always brings pleasure. The fulfillment of the drive sometimes comes ambivalently mixed with anguish or anxiety or even acute pain. Take the fulfillment of a sexual maniac: he is not so rare in our society as to be dismissed as an exception that need not be considered. As these pages were first being written the papers were carrying news of the last of five murderous assaults on girls near Ann Arbor. Not only is the sexual maniac not rare but he is the extreme instance of a condition that is manifest in others to an extent that does not lead to flight from the police or to prison. Take the case of a man like Crippen, or better yet, a man like Heirens. The latter seems to have been driven to murder irresistibly, and the appearance of the drive seems to have corresponded with the appearance of a different personality from that of the brilliant undergraduate that he normally was. Those of us who read the newspapers when the case was horrifying the nation remember that he wrote with lipstick on the wall of the apartment of one of his victims, asking to be caught lest he continue to kill. One can guess that the Jekyll-Hyde conflict, at the moment of his writing on the wall, must have been intensely painful. The fulfillment of his end could not be said to have been pleasure *tout court*, and the result of his short career of crime, a life sentence he is still serving, cannot be called happiness.

To sharpen the issue, let us overlook the ambivalence, for evidence to the contrary prohibits the assumption that it is a concomitant of every sexual murder. Allow, what sometimes seems to be the case, that an ineffable euphoria lasting for days, follows the sexual murder. Let us imagine that a sexual criminal is outfitted with Gyges ring, which by a turn on the finger makes him invisible. Add, contrary to fact, that he is entirely devoid of any feeling towards his fellowmen. I say "contrary to fact," because it is my understanding that no totally amoral person, morally totally anaesthetic, has ever been encountered. Our man goes through life murdering women and successfully evading the police. This would mean, not a short career, but a life-long one of intense and frequent pleasure. Could one call such a man happy? Certainly, if happiness were solely constituted by intense and frequent pleasure. One often runs into cocky logicians in introductory courses in philosophy who assert that such a man would be happy. The conclusion follows verbally from the premises, but we can see clearly that the term "happy" cannot quite mean intense and frequent pleasure in sexual murder.

Of course the example does not apply to Marcuse, for whom happiness is social (he would say "societal," thus increasing the depth of his thought). But the point is not that Marcuse ought to agree with the cocky logician. The point is that pleasure and happiness and morality cannot be connected simplistically, and that the man who believes that the good life consists of happiness conceived as the successful enjoyment of pleasure and avoidance of pain, in a social context, advocates a doctrine that has no solid anchorage on the facts of human experience. The song and dance about polymorphous and narcissistic resexualization, when examined, reminds one of the picture coarse-minded factualists have of philosophers—men levitated above "the fury and the mire of human veins." A life cannot be called good that is a continuous hell of unrelenting pain and frustration. But neither can one be called good that is a continuous, uninterrupted enjoyment of pleasure and nothing else. The cloying sweetness of it would drive many men into insanity. Not all men, however: I had the good fortune once of knowing a true hedonist. "Good" because I learned a lot from him about men. His capacity for pleasure of various kinds apparently had no limits in intensity and duration.

Numerous other phenomena would have to be analyzed

144

before we could claim a right to a firm opinion regarding the sources of pleasure and the relation of pleasure to happiness. I shall cite briefly a number of these phenomena, keeping the analysis to the minimum required to make clear what the problems consist in. Unless we are to accept the tenet that upon becoming polymorphously resexualized we are not going to be burdened any longer with mental illness, we need more knowledge than we have of the relationship of neuroses to pleasure and unpleasure. We also need to know whether the correlations that have been proposed between the need for pleasure and the individual's somatotype are as well founded as those who advocate the correlations take them to be.

An adequate consideration of pleasure and happiness would also have to indicate attention to the problem posed by men who buck the mores of the group to which they belong: the mild dissenter, the fanatical revolutionist or religious reformer: a John Huss, a John Smith, a Rosa Luxemburg. These people turn themselves deliberately into means in order to achieve ends which, not infrequently, they do not expect to see realized during their lifetime. They use themselves, body and mind, they turn their wives, sons, daughters, parents, friends into tools, with less concern for themselves and their human instruments than an ordinary worker shows for his tools. The energy, the dedication to values to be enjoyed by others, the self-sacrifice involved—what relation exactly do these factors have to pleasure and happiness? We cannot say of these people that they are sick. In error no doubt some of them were or are; but sick, necessarily? If Marcuse holds, as he seems to, that men ought to strive after happiness for themselves as well as for the rest of mankind, one is not altogether a good man who, in seeking happiness for others, gives up altogether the chance of happiness for himself.

This theme was suggested by Marcuse himself when he told us in the last paragraph of *One-Dimensional Man* that his "critical theory" wants to remain loyal to those who, without hope, have given and give their lives to the Great Refusal. We cannot allow that Marcuse wrote this threnody carelessly. Without hope: that means the Great Refusers did not, and do

145

not, expect to see the day when Marcuse's dystopia will be inaugurated; it means that they knew and know that it will never be realized. They give their lives for principles and values that remain for them a vision and no more. How then can we say that they derive pleasure by identifying themselves with men who will be happy because of their sacrifices when they know such men will never be? There are other motives, it would seem, besides pleasure, to prompt us to action that cannot now or ever promise pleasure.

There are other complications we must touch on. Aside from the obvious heterogeneity of our capacity to enjoy pleasure and of our need for it, there is the problem of the kinds of pleasure men want. Let us begin by remembering that pleasure *qua* pleasure, pleasure considered as purely psychological or subjective experience, in abstraction from the stimulus that elicits it, differs only in intensity and duration from other pleasures equally considered in abstraction from their stimuli and viewed solely in their subjective, psychological aspect. But here, first, a verbal difficulty must be overcome. The word "experience" has two different, though related, meanings. We might call these a broad and a narrow meaning. The one may legitimately be used to refer to the purely subjective, inward, or merely psychological events that take place when a stimulus acts upon us, in abstraction from the stimulus that sets them going. Or it may be used to refer to the whole situation, to a subject reacting to a stimulus. The latter meaning can be formulated as the following relational complex: [s - R - o], in which obviously the s is the psychological organism, the subject; the o the stimulating object; and the R the relation that turns an o into a stimulus for an s. The claim I am making is that experiences of pleasure, in abstraction from the relational complexes in which they occur, the s's alone, do not differ from one another in kind by virtue of their felt qualities. In a number of relational complexes of pleasure $[s - R - o]_1$, $[s - R - o]_2$, $[s - R - o]_3$, $[s - R - o]_4$, ... $[s - R - o]_n$, one whole relational complex differs from the others in kind, insofar as the o's differ from one another; the different o's give the relational complexes of pleasure a different felt quality in each case. But the s's in abstrac-

146

tion from the o's, and therefore the R's that relate the o's to the s's, differ from one another solely in quantity, which is to say in intensity and duration. I am speaking of the felt quality of the subjective or purely psychological experience, for no one would wish to deny that different organs are involved in the different pleasures that are elicited by a different stimulus.

Since Marcuse holds that the pleasures men seek must be distinguished in kind, for there are true or vital pleasures and false ones, it should be readily seen that his theory is incoherent. He cannot do justice to the pleasures elicited by diverse objects, because he has no other criterion for quality than the pleasure the object elicits. Since pleasure *qua* pleasure differs only quantitatively, and pleasure is the only criterion, there is, in his view, no ground for preferring Bach concerts to a big car. Hence, the distinction he makes between some pleasures and others, called spiritual, finds no support in his hedonistic doctrine.

But above all the notion of happiness is an empty notion when coupled with a drive psychology. And so, to some extent, is pleasure. As Marcuse knows, one cannot seek happiness. One man is interested in one object and another man is interested in another object. Marcuse is interested in two objects: in the destruction of our society and in dreaming about a dystopia that not only seems improbable but disgusting to many men. If the interest in the contemplation of the achievement of the first of these objects and in the vague dream of the second give him happiness, he is a happy man, and nothing more can be said. But in order to be happy through polymorphous and narcissistic regression to the childish condition prior to the dominance of the genital, one needs to be interested in so regressing, and a number of the considerations preceding have shown that the belief that all men would be interested in regressing to a pregenital state is built on assumptions that he has not established.

Although one cannot seek happiness, one can seek pleasure, —although an object is always involved, if it be only the resexualized body that has regressed to a stage prior to the genital.

147

However, it has long been known, and few would deny it today, that the pursuit of pleasure for its own sake, the steady chase of pleasure *qua* pleasure, soon betrays the seeker. The man dedicated to the exclusive enjoyment of pleasure ends in boredom and not infrequently in the throttling emptiness of despair.

I have dealt with the problems of psychological hedonism in order to bring out with some clarity what I take to be the human irresponsibility of the revolutionist, his profound immorality. We must next turn to the question, on what grounds can universalistic ethical hedonism be advocated? Although Marcuse's essay "On Hedonism" was written seventeen years before *Eros and Civilization,* nowhere in it, or later so far as I know, does he discuss the basis of universalistic ethical hedonism. A discussion of this topic would supply us with an answer to the question: Why ought one to seek happiness through pleasure for all men?

Insofar as Marcuse assumes the answer to be obvious, he is neither a negative thinker nor an original one. In this respect he is merely one of a large multitude of people—scholars, thinkers, religious people and others—who accept unexamined the popular orthodoxy of our age. The difference between Marcuse and his fellow secularists is that for a number of reasons the large majority of orthodox secularists do not dare push their position to its logical conclusion, whereas Marcuse, a socialist, a sort of Freudian, and up to recently quite indifferent to the impression his views created on those of his readers who are prudent and conventional, does not hesitate to push his hedonism as far as it will go.

Although there is no logical connection between materialism —whether dialectical or earlier or later-day atomistic—and ethical hedonism, it is psychologically reasonable that a materialist should be a hedonist. For materialists are naturalists in the cosmological sense. One of their tenets is that values are products of human desires or interests. The universe itself, viewed independently of human desires or interests is, as it is put in the language of the schools, "value-free." The Marxist traces the presence of values to class interests and conflicts. But what is the point of defending our interests if they are irrelevant to human well-being? And what in the last analysis is human well-being, but a sustained condition of pleasure which is called happiness for the individual and the community? And how are we to enjoy pleasure if it is not us, you, me, Tom and Dick and Herb and the others, who enjoy it? And what ultimately is pleasure, if it is not an experience enjoyed by each of us in or through our bodies?

Marcuse includes in the class of pleasures those he calls "spiritual." He notes that there are other pleasures besides those enjoyed through "the reactivation of all [the] erotogenic zones" of the body, and adds that "nothing in the nature of Eros" justifies the notion that pleasure is to be confined to the corporeal sphere only. (*E & C*, p. 210) The reactivation of pregenital polymorphous sexuality, and the decline of genital supremacy would open the "spiritual sphere" to enjoyment. A journalist who interviewed Marcuse when he returned to San Diego after the threat on his life told us that Marcuse enjoys good food, good wine, good cigars, good company and good music. But this does not tell us what Marcuse could possibly mean by "spiritual," for even music can be a purely or a dominantly erotic enjoyment—and the word "erotic" is used here in its popular sense. Havelock Ellis mentions in one of the volumes of his *Studies in the Psychology of Sex*—I am confident that my memory does not betray me on this point, although it is fifty years since I read him—that there are people who respond to music orgasmically. I knew two women who did. But even if this mode of response were some form of peculiar response to be discounted, we could still demand to be told what the word "spiritual" means to a materialist. Marcuse may be working here at a disadvantage. He may have in mind a distinction I shall dwell on below between *geistig* and *geistlich* for which English has no comparable terms.

But let us pose the question again and ask, can we accept pleasure as happiness to be the end of man? The question that is being raised is that of ethical hedonism, according to which sustained pleasure ought to be the goal of our activities. For as I pointed out above, I have to assume, although I cannot be fully confident of my assumption, that Marcuse is both a psychological and universalistic ethical hedonist.

As a moral theory I find ethical hedonism inadmissible. But considered in abstraction from a total view of man and the universe, particularly those aspects of man's activity that involve radical moral conflicts, I know of only one argument against the doctrine and that is the Kantian argument I used against it in a book on moral philosophy published in 1951—interestingly enough it is the very passage quoted by Marcuse in his essay "On Hedonism" in another connection. I transcribe the complete paragraph I used then:

> But that there is any intrinsic worth in the real existence of a man who merely lives for *enjoyment,* however busy he may be in this respect, even when in so doing he serves others—all equally with himself intent only on enjoyment—as an excellent means to that one end, and does so, moreover, because through sympathy he shares all their gratifications,—this is a view to which reason will never let itself be brought round. Only by what a man does heedless of enjoyment, in complete freedom and independently of what he can procure passively from the hand of nature, does he give to his existence, as the real existence of a person, an absolute worth. Happiness, with all its plethora of pleasures, is far from being an unconditioned good.

This statement is to be found in the *Critique of Aesthetic Judgment,* translated by James Creed Meredith (Oxford, 1911, pp. 47-48). It sounds as if it were based on intuition, but I do not believe it is. It is an "inference" from—a "deduction" or the drawing of one of the consequences of—a view of man, as Marcuse's is an inference—or deduction, or drawing of the consequences of—a different view of man, totally in contradiction to Kant's. While I do not subscribe to Kant's view of man—his Eighteenth Century rationalism, his rigid table of categories, his profound pietism, and his categorical imperative as I understand it, besides much else, of perhaps lesser importance, prevent me—I have deep sympathy and respect for it.

Another consideration must be brought forward against ethical hedonism. Let me present it in a roundabout way. Marcuse has said that he does not want to see our technology destroyed. And it is obvious why this should be the case. Without it it would not be possible to feed the millions that now crowd the earth. But he has never considered the conditions needed to maintain the present level of technological efficiency we have achieved. Could men consistently dedicated to the pursuit of pleasure maintain our technology? I do not ask whether they could create it, but whether they could maintain it; for to create it ruthless self-sacrifice was required, that men consistently devoted to playing and displaying are not likely to exercise. But could consistent hedonists even maintain a technological society? Overlook the likelihood that it may not be possible to maintain our technology without constantly adding to it by the application of creative effort to science and engineering, that to seek merely to maintain it would bring about a regress. But overlook this possibility. Merely to maintain a technological society some degree of rigorous ascesis is required. That we may not be aware of the ascesis called for to run our technology is not surprising: we are used to it, we are no more aware of it than we are of the atmospheric pressure under which we live. In order to see how much ascesis is exercised by the majority of us all we need do is compare in our minds the relatively relaxed existence of a primitive society with our habits of work: the demands of effort, of punctuality, of abstention from immediate ease for the sake of order, the need for planning and carrying out the plans, the sense of social responsibility, the selflessness—these are habits (I shall not call them virtues) all of which do not seem to be compatible with the self-indulgence which is the constitutive trait of the hedonist.

It seems to me fair to conclude that before we are in a position to assert that men ought to seek happiness through pleasure we have to undertake a protracted and complex analysis of man's nature, of the problem of moral obligation, and particularly we must undertake to prove that pleasure has the

151

primacy above all other goals men ought to seek. This analysis Marcuse does not undertake. We are free therefore to conclude that his hedonistic imperative is not binding on us.

Marcuse's defender will retort: "You have been discussing man in a repressive society; and since you took a personal stand against hedonists and utilitarians I feel free to tell you that you talk the way you do because you have been misshaped by the system that instills in its flunkies abhorrence of pleasure as an end in itself. Marcuse is not thinking about yesterday or today. He is not thinking about the actual societies that have existed or exist. And you know it. He is speaking about what man will be like when, breaking his shackles, he will rise in full freedom to play and display." My answer to this defense has already been put down from a different standpoint. It is that the only man I can think about is the talking animal that has been around, as of the latest expert guess, for about one hundred and fifty thousand years, give or take a few millennia. He presents us with an extremely difficult problem into which it would be most interesting to go in full detail. It adds up to this: For all we know about man, the richness of his allotropic manifestations, his capacity for adaptation, his great virtues and ugly vices, his need for knowledge and his incurable credulity, essentially we know very little about man. Our lack of knowledge is the result of the many contradictory theories we have. From these we cannot eliminate the false ones or bring to genuine synthesis those that seem valid. We do not even know which are which.

But we seem to know this: When man became human, or *as* he was becoming, he took on a heavy burden that became so closely woven in with his purely utilitarian inventions for adaptation and survival that it does not seem possible to separate the one from the others. His diverse customs consist often of backbreaking taboos, restraints, and inhibitions that, being self-imposed, one would say—and rationalists do say—could easily be thrown off. But neither in fact nor in principle can man lay this burden down. At this point two observations are essential if we are to understand man at all: From the outside of the group a system of taboos seems quite irrational. Sometimes it seems to be the product of whimsey, invented by man in order to create difficulties for himself, as if he were miserable to the degree that he is freed from misery. Why should a family have to call in a *goy* to light the gas on the Sabbath? Putting a match to a gas jet is no work. But neither is abstaining from meat on Fridays, as was done by prescription to large numbers of people until recently.

From the outside few taboos make any sense. But from the inside, it turns out that these self-imposed burdens are the very ligaments and muscles that keep individuals and groups going, that give them the morale needed to handle with some chance of success the vicissitudes met with in a world always harsh. Take them away in order to lighten man's burden and to make his going easier, and he bobs up and down in the choppy sea, incapable of keeping a course and in danger of turning over. Men have always fought for ideals. But to Sovereign Reason some of these are mad, destructive, fantastic. And yet, what would man be if he were stripped of his dreams and his burdens? It is in this man, the man of flesh and bone, about whom I know from the little history I have read, and whom I have seen, by direct contact or by account, in my own wretched world, that I am interested. The speculative, a priori, abstract, "rational" picture of Man dreamt by a lover of Man who hates men, or by any other peddler of secular *Erlösungslehre,* is interesting for what it tells of the dreamer. About the men of flesh and bone of which I know a little, a number of other things can also be said.

Among the things I believe we can say is that Marcuse's faith in a possible happiness achieved under his "rational" guidance is to many of us utterly inadmissible and, to some, nauseating. Marcuse, by the way, calls his faith "the propositions of philosophical anthropology," as if there were only one such discipline, as there is only one Euclidean geometry and as if he had a corner on it. But let that be. A sufficient reason for rejecting Marcuse's freedom from the tyranny of the genital is that in doing so we would be placing a bet at unacceptable odds. Destroy what we have, because of its faults, he urges us, and build a good world. We acknowledge

153

the faults. But we remember that our system is self-corrective, and that its instrumentalities work more or less poorly, but work. We are asked to wreck this world of ours in order to bring about a vague dream which tells us nothing but that we shall play and display with a minimum of labor. Marcuse presents it as a pleasant and attractive vision. But when I look at it critically, and consider what I know of Marcuse's doctrine besides its repugnant hedonism, when I become aware of the tyrannical rasping undertone of his program, I become more and more alarmed. What we have is bad enough. What we are promised, insofar as we can make it out through the verbiage and the apodictic self-confidence in the propositions of his philosophical anthropology, is not to be taken seriously. What we must take seriously is the temper that animates the argument.

Marcuse is not only an ethical hedonist, as already noted, but he is a universalistic hedonist. This means that he recommends that we ought to seek, not only our personal happiness, but each the happiness of the rest of mankind. He writes:

> The first goal of struggle is only a particular social group's interest in better, more humane conditions of life. But this particular interest cannot be pursued without bettering and making more humane the conditions of life of the whole and liberating the entire society (*N*, p. 195).

Take this other statement:

> That the true interest of individuals is the interest of freedom, that true individual freedom can co-exist with real general freedom and, indeed, is possible only in conjunction with it, that happiness ultimately consists in freedom—these are not propositions of philosophical anthropology about the nature of man but descriptions of a historical situation which humanity has achieved for itself in the struggle with nature (p. 192).

There are numerous other expressions throughout his work of his concern for all the exploited and the needy, the underprivileged of the whole world. Bishop Butler explained with great subtlety, acuity and prudence what we must understand by the commandment "Love thy neighbor as thyself." The question is as to whom must we consider our neighbor. Not the whole of mankind, said Butler. But it might be brought up against Butler that he was living in the insular world of his Eighteenth Century, with its notion of universal man gained from information gathered from the parish. It was given to Marx to see that we are all neighbors, including Papuans in valleys as yet unvisited.

One could use up a large number of pages commenting in detail on the several propositions put forth in these two quotations. For instance, in view of the way men seem to be eager to give up their freedom to despots and demagogues in exchange for promissory notes whose only collateral is the rhetoric in which they are offered, on what grounds does Marcuse say that the true interest of the individual is the interest in freedom? The proposition holds against all evidence contrary to it because Marcuse controls the meaning of "true" and of "interest," stipulating what is true and what is false. But factually it is not true that men are interested in freedom. In the absence of a head count and a careful historical investigation, it would seem that Ivan Karamazov's Grand Inquisitor was right when he reproached Jesus for wanting to give people a freedom which they did not want. Here and there, in limited respects, and perhaps only in the West, if my ignorance does not betray me, men have wanted and fought for freedom and enjoyed it for brief moments. In the United States men have enjoyed some freedoms even before the founding of the republic, and considerably more afterwards. But it is clear that they are losing their freedoms and that not many seem concerned over the loss. In this case the Grand Inquisitor's view seems to hold. Nor can there be any doubt that, should Marcuse's party triumph, the freedoms enjoyed by the American people would be ruthlessly and repressively "tolerated." But Marcuse is not really interested in man's freedom or freedoms. He is interested in man's freedom to regress, whether he wants it or not, to a state of polymorphic and narcissistic sexuality. And what that freedom means, when you look at it in detail,

155

we have already seen is Marcuse's freedom to force us to be the kind of men he has decided we ought to be. I have detained myself on this question in order to reinforce a criticism already made in these pages several times. It adds up to the fact that Marcuse is not interested in facts or in distinctions between how things are and cannot help but be on the one side and how, according to him, they ought to be.

But why can't we be truly happy unless all men are happy? To this important question Marcuse does not address himself. He merely asserts this to be the case. But the proposition is not at all self-evident. It would seem that the contrary is the case. It seems that men can be happy and enjoy a good deal of pleasure, and enjoy it permanently, while others, and not those living in the antipodes but in the house next to them, are suffering and are known to be suffering. Because one man's suffering would spoil another's pleasure and happiness? This is a question of *fact*. Lucretius did not think so; rather he thought the very opposite. And Lucretius was a thoughtful man although a hedonist. Lucretius aside, it would seem that there are vast variations among people in this respect, and that the variations may range between those who cannot crush an ant or step on a worm, at one end of the band, and those at the other end who are utterly indifferent to the pain of living things, whether brutes or human beings. Men sensitive to the pain of others are not necessarily sentimental, nor are they like Tolstoy's countess who cries in the theatre while her coachman freezes. To the empirical question, then, the answer may be: Whether a man can enjoy pleasure and happiness while others are deprived of these goods depends on his imagination, his capacity for feeling his human ties with other human beings, his moral refinement, and a number of other such qualities, as to whose source and capacity for development we do not know much.

There is another observation to be made. As already suggested, Marcuse's doctrine seems to be irrefutable, since it depends on what he means by "true happiness." If true happiness includes our knowledge that there are no unhappy ones on the whole earth and false happiness our indifference to others, then it is clear that we cannot be truly happy unless we meet the conditions of the definition. But the definition is irrelevant to the actual natures of men and quite arbitrary. "True happiness," however, could mean that for a man to be happy he must develop his capacities to the full, and that among these must be included his capacity to love—in the Christian sense—mankind and not merely his neighbors. This is a meaningful proposition but not one into whose development and proof Marcuse enters.

Let me broach this theme from a different angle. There may be some general conditions for man's happiness—good health, absence of frustration, even if the wishes satisfied are anti-social, a modicum of satisfaction in the work he does, and a number of others that probably apply to men anywhere whom we may justifiably call happy. But happiness is an individual matter, to be enjoyed not in general terms but in terms of the individual's specific needs, character, and physical and moral endowment. A set of conditions that make one man happy will make another unhappy. The variables here would have to be analyzed with care before we indulge in speculative generalizations and arbitrary prescriptions.

I shall name a few of the variables, merely to show the complexity of the problem. A man's capacity for happiness, if we are talking of actual happiness and not a happiness prescribed from the outside by a despotic chiliast, may depend on his indifference to the suffering of others or, on the contrary, on the depth and breadth of his moral imagination, on his sense of human brotherhood or on the hardness of his heart. A neurosis may turn a man into a monad incapable of reflecting the universe or into an oversensitive conscience burdened by irrational anxiety and self-destructive concern for others.

Philosophers writing about happiness are not describing the real McCoy. They are usually objectifying their yearnings. Actual happiness, not the dreams of the philosophers, if it means anything, depends on so many purely idiosyncratic factors that it must always be treated casuistically. I have known people who seemed to be relatively happy, but whose concern for their fellow beings was limited: I know of happy marriages, say, in

157

which the head of the family was doing rewarding work and the wife was not bored by running a home and taking care of the children. These people do not suffer from chronic frustration, or irremediable misfortunes. These people give to organized charity, vote, are good neighbors, know that their society is not perfect but know that many of its imperfections are in the process of correction while others are under indictment. They seem to others, and consider themselves to be, relatively happy and relatively free. And yet, according to Marcuse they are not, cannot be, and ought not to be. Why not? If we do not believe we are brothers under a Providential Father or, lacking such a belief, we do not believe in the doctrine of axiological realism—the doctrine that holds that values have status in being independently of those who espouse them or recognize them—I do not see why we cannot be happy and at the same time be hypocritical stinkers who know how to get by.

Why should I have feelings, capacities, and sensitive responses I now lack? Because everybody ought to be happy and without these qualities I make others unhappy. But everybody ought to be happy. Everybody? Do you include those I hate too? One reason—among many others—I cannot call myself a Christian is that I have in my life hated with consuming hatred two men, hated them intensely and still do. One is dead. The other flourishes. Do I have to make this man happy before I can be happy? As Cambronne did not say, *Merde*. His happiness makes me unhappy, and that is the reason I try not to think of him.

Ah. How wrong can one be? For in Marcuse's utopia we shall not hate anyone. No one at all? Well, maybe a few, but not intensely, just a bit only. "Struggle with nature and even among men continues" in the future, he tells us. But it will be quite different from what it is now since, "In his relation to the authentic general interest, the individual would relate to truth; the demands and decisions of the whole would then preserve the individual [sic] interest and eventually promote his happiness." (*N*, p. 193) That being the case, the kind of animosity and hatred that exists today and poisons our lives would tend to disappear, and even Marcuse would find that his own vitriolic hatred would drain off. These are Marcuse's own words:

> When all present subjective and objective potentialities of development have been unbound, the needs and wants themselves [those we now have, that is] will change. Those based on social compulsion or repression, on injustice, and on filth and poverty would necessarily disappear. There may still be the sick, the insane, and the criminal . . . Particular interest will not coincide immediately with true interest. *(Loc. cit.)*

No, not immediately. But in the long run it will. Given sufficient force and Marcuse's doctrine of repressive tolerance, those whose interests do not coincide with the needs of Marcuse and his boys will indeed disappear.

With some qualifications that need not be put on record here, Marcuse's doctrine is acceptable. But note first that he did not originate the doctrine he advocates; in the West, it goes back to Jesus and the prophets, on one line of development, and on another, to the Stoics. Personal happiness, to be enduring, to be full, rich, self-satisfying, to have depth and resonance throughout one's daily pinpricks and the less frequent hammer blows, cannot be egoistic; it must extend beyond the narrow confines of the self and include the well-being of others. Notice, also, that I have put the doctrine in my own terms. And having agreed to the general formulation of the doctrine, the question would immediately arise about the extent of its coverage and the degrees of concern with which it applies to "our neighbors" in Bishop Butler's sense, or to mankind in the socialist sense. In view of the small world in which we have to live today, it would seem as if each of us would be better off if no one were suffering from gratuitous and premeditated malevolence. But this reason for behaving with kindness towards our fellows is merely utilitarian, and suffers from all the defects that have been brought up against utilitarianism. In practice, the doctrine is contingent upon circumstances, which qualify and reduce its universal application.

159

If it is assumed, as it is by Marcuse throughout, explicitly or implicitly, that the society he would destroy is all wrong, there is no problem: our society deserves no mercy. But in his last book and in a published interview he qualified his condemnation. The qualification in turn invalidates the indictment. In any case, his condemnation, when unqualified, arises from a rancor that makes him blind to the factual evidence.

As important as these considerations are, it should also be noted with full candor and appropriate emphasis that Marcuse's world is a Darwinian, might-makes-right world, in which tolerance is shown only towards those who agree with him and liquidation would be the fate of those who disagree, had his side the power. In such a world, the judgment that it is wrong for us to defend ourselves loses all meaning. Moral judgments across warring armies are meaningless. From Marcuse's standpoint we are wrong. But we do not take his standpoint, and he has no means of forcing us to take it. He could liquidate us if he had the power, but he could not convince us. When war begins, morality is put in storage for the duration, and the only reason either side refrains from carrying on without restraint is prudence of the lowest order: fear of reprisals. On Marcuse's partisan morality, his condemnation cannot reach us. He judges us wrong—we know that, and laugh at him. For his judgment is only valid for those who agree with him.

But besides the utilitarian ground for agreeing with Marcuse, once I am permitted to reformulate his thesis I have reasons for espousing the doctrine that he cannot appeal to. My notion of the person—a category which transcends the range of psychology and of social interrelationships, and has its proper roots in the metaphysics of axiological realism—compels me to espouse the value of the other, irrespective of party, class, declared warfare or any other kind of social divisions. Let me hasten to add that this espousal of the value of the person does not make me a pacifist. But here I must stop. All that needs be emphasized at this juncture is that Marcuse's doctrine offers him no means of resolving radical moral conflicts morally. Without such means he has no answer to the speech made by the Athenian ambassadors to the citizens of Melos. The strong exact what they can; the weak yield what they must. But a thinker who provides no means of resolving radical moral conflicts morally is appealing to something he calls "morality" but that is, in fact, another one of his weapons for carrying on the war he is engaged in, and a weapon that is used to destroy the enemy, not to uphold justice or truth if these terms apply to objective relationships. This is what Marcuse does. It is seen clearly in his doctrine, as it is in nearly all ethical theory advanced by contemporary thinkers. His outrage and his pity have no moral tint. They are reactions strictly reserved for his side, he would not waste them on his enemies.

I turn to the problem of method. The essays translated into English in *Negations* and published in German in
New York in the Thirties were explicitly antagonistic to empiricism. Of late Marcuse has claimed that contentions of his
are "empirical." I do not want to call attention to a contradiction, for it is clear that he has changed his mind about
method. What we must examine is whether his appeal to experience can be validated.

Let me begin by calling attention to the fact that Marcuse
has learned very little from his American experience. Unlike
the German refugees whose minds were deepened by their life
in the United States—Cassirer is to my mind the best example
—Marcuse does not seem to have felt the need to pick up much
that American scholarship had to offer him. In the introduction

162

to *One-Dimensional Man* Marcuse gives credit to a number of writers to whom he is indebted. Among them, he tells us, he would like to emphasize "the vital importance of the work of C. W. Mills," and he mentions in a mildly apologetic manner his debt to Vance Packard, William W. Whyte, and Fred J. Cook. Why the manner? Probably because he knows that these partisan journalists have no standing as scientists.

In the following paragraphs I direct the reader's attention to Marcuse's lamentably exiguous knowledge of the history of philosophy and his misconception of empiricism. I do not have to go again over his empirical irresponsibility. In the discussion of his conception of the role of art I called attention to this fault. I also called attention to it, in an implicit way, in the discussion of his view of the tyranny of the genital; and quite explicitly in our discussion of needs and drives, because of Marcuse's failure to take account of the facts of cultural pluralism. Indeed, in its application, what Marcuse's purely speculative method adds up to is the *ad hoc* manufacture of evidence or the systematic ignoring of facts in order to further his indictment.

It should be observed, however, that I am not the only critic who has called attention to these defects. In a book already referred to, *The Freudian Left* (pp. 166 ff.), Robinson takes up this matter as well as Marcuse's animus towards naturalism. As regards the latter, there is no need to say much. In the Thirties Marcuse used to attack naturalism, but he could not really have been attacking what American philosophers call naturalism, for as a Marxist and a Freudian Marcuse was and is as much of a naturalist as any thinker living today. A naturalist is a man who believes that there are no factors or agencies outside of nature required to explain or account for any event or phenomenon in nature. But contemporary naturalists tacked onto this basic tenet the added tenet that the best way to understand events or phenomena was by the application of the method—they seldom wrote, "methods"—of science. What I suspect Marcuse was objecting to when he attacked naturalism was its militant attachment to the methods of science, which is to say, its ineradicable empiricism. But naturalism need not

163

be tied up with either empiricism, science, or scientism. It can be rationalistic, as Spinoza's naturalism was. What Marcuse must have objected to in the Thirties must have been the rejection by the majority of American philosophers of the phenomenological method.

In his *Marcuse* (p. 19) Alasdair MacIntyre criticizes our negative critic's "dubious" history of philosophy and his even more dubious general history of culture. I concur. His faulty knowledge of the history of philosophy I am about to exhibit to the reader. For Marcuse's dubious knowledge of the general history of culture I shall let MacIntyre's statement stand, without further discussion.

The statement, however, that Marcuse has learned very little from his American experience must be qualified and documented. Between the essays written in the Thirties in the United States and the essay on "Repressive Tolerance" and the short book *An Essay on Liberation,* there is a change in his thinking that must be noted and may be attributed to his American sojourn. The phenomenological method is, at least outwardly, abandoned. If he does not become an empiricist in the thorough-paced way in which American sociologists—as distinct from propagandists—are, today he no longer claims that essences appear on the face of what actually exists. In the Thirties he attacked empiricism because he believed that it upheld the *status quo.* What he understood by empiricism, however, was the classical "empirical epistemology" of the British philosophers, particularly of Locke and Hume, to whom he refers explicitly. Against empiricism, with its alleged subservience to facts as they are, he sets up "reason" by which, as we shall see below, he understands something other than we understand today.

About Marcuse's treatment of empiricism the following observations are called for: The first is that in rejecting the classical empiricism of Locke and Hume he uses a technique he employs throughout, of shooting with a sawed-off shotgun. Thus he does not notice that Locke could be called not only an empiricist but also something of a Cartesian rationalist, and must be thought of as one of the ancestors of contemporary

164

liberal, if not radical, tendencies. He justified philosophically the revolution of 1688. Hume was indeed a conservative in politics. But to call Hume a conservative *tout court* is demonstrably to disregard the historical facts. Had Hume been a conservative all of one piece he would not have rudely awakened Kant from his Leibnizian-Wolfian siesta. Hume's reductive analysis of the self into impressions blasted the foundations of the belief in immortality; his morality was utilitarian and at the time, therefore, an unsettling force rather than a conservative one; and his analysis of cause threatened, as Kant took it, the foundations of the physics of the day. In matters of theology Hume was, to put it politely, systematically ambiguous, and historians are still arguing about what exactly he believed. But this much is certain: Hume did not give comfort to orthodox Christianity—and this is putting it minimally.

Marcuse also fails to notice that Seventeenth- and Eighteenth-Century empiricism could with justification be hailed as "progressive" since it allied itself with the science of the day against traditional philosophy. The *philosophes* welcomed it. And Hume states explicitly in *An Enquiry Concerning the Principles of Morals* that in his search for the foundation of ethics and those universal principles from which all censure or approbation derives, he is going to use, not abstract science but the experimental method. If we take the whole picture into consideration, and if we take it in its historical context, we see that Locke and Hume were, on the whole, fulfilling what Marcuse calls "the historical task of philosophy" which, as we have seen, he lays down to be "the intellectual dissolution and even subversion of the given facts."

Just as important is the fact that in his dismissal of empiricism Marcuse confines his attack to what has been called "empiricism" in histories of philosophy, the classical British empiricism, and does not look beyond the label. But empiricism did not stop with Hume whose empiricism, anyway, was far less "empirical" than he took it to be. Marcuse ignores Bentham and John Stuart Mill, although both were empiricists even if they have been called utilitarians. And he overlooks entirely contemporary empiricism, both American and English. But

Russell, in the days when he used to philosophize, was an empiricist and the American philosophical scene of the first third of this century and even later was crowded with all kinds of empiricists, although usually labeled either pragmatists, or naturalists, or realists. Men like Dewey, Sellars *père*, Woodbridge, Morris Cohen (with a slight qualification), Meade, E. B. McGilvary, and the Santayana of *The Life of Reason*—the fifth volume of which, *Reason in Science*, presented for the day an almost positivistic version of science and its method—and Prall. Very few American empiricists could be called "conservative." The majority were progressive or liberal, and one of them at least, Sellars, flirted openly with the Bolshies as late as the Forties. Before Prall died, there were rumors about his connections with Stalinism. The rumors do not prove that he was a Stalinist. But they certainly give one reason to believe that he was no conservative.

These instances point out in concrete terms what can be argued in abstract terms, namely that there is no logical connection between contemporary empiricism and political affiliations any more than there was between classical empiricism and the politics of Locke and Hume. The fundamental reason for the lack of logical connection between empiricism, whether as total philosophy or as epistemological doctrine or as scientific method, and a political theory is that the empiricist was never committed to the belief in the inviolability of the social reality, which, if he was empirical, he saw as in flux. At most, what from his point of view Marcuse has a right to bring against empirical social science, and he does indeed bring it up, is that it tries, or used to try, to be value-free. Whether it ever succeeded in being value-free or not is another question. But there is no doubt that until the recent declarations by New Left so-called "social scientists" in favor of subjectivism and against the ideal of objectivity, social science tried as hard as it could to be objective, value-free. There is another reason for the fundamental lack of connection between empiricism and any one political doctrine. That is that all empiricists claim to look at the facts, but the facts that the social sciences look at are not given in the way in which they are in the so-called hard

166

sciences. This is all the more the case in respect to social valuations, whether formulated by the scientist or observed and reported by him.

The animus against empiricism remains with Marcuse up to and including *One-Dimensional Man,* for the previous book, *Eros and Civilization,* was a purely speculative exercise. In the writer of *One-Dimensional Man* one would expect respect for the facts. After all, he is criticizing the alleged condition of a nation. But whatever name we can give his method, "empirical" it cannot be called.

But in two recent publications, "Repressive Tolerance" in *A Critique of Pure Tolerance,* and in *An Essay on Liberation,* Marcuse appeals to empiricism. In "Repressive Tolerance" he writes: "I suggested that the distinction between true and false tolerance, between progress and regression can be made rationally on empirical grounds." (p. 105) Here reason and the empirical facts are not in opposition to each other. And on the next page he repeats the thought: "However, granted the empirical rationality of the distinction between progress and regression . . ." In *An Essay on Liberation* he tells us that "Negative thinking draws whatever force it may have from its empirical basis." (p. 87) Although the attitude towards empiricism seems to have changed, let me repeat that Marcuse has never really shown respect for empirical data and does not yet. For him the term "the given facts" is a term of excoriation, since it usually refers to the social reality of today and not of the millenarian future he envisages. Facts are frequently roadblocks for his either/or thinking; they give the lie to his simplistic dichotomies. Facts, therefore, are better made up than gathered.

Marcuse is not only given to thinking in generalities and unanchored abstractions, but he affirms that he believes this is the only way to think authentically. In *One-Dimensional Man* he has penned a panegyric to abstract thought. He holds that philosophy originates in a dissociation from practice—which was probably the case in Ionia and in India. And he continues:

167

By virtue of this dissociation, critical philosophic thought is necessarily transcendent and *abstract.* Philosophy shares this abstractness with all genuine thought, for nobody really thinks who does not abstract from that which is given, who does not relate the facts to the factors which have made them, who does not—in his mind—undo the facts. Abstractness is the very life of thought, the token of its authenticity. (*O-D M,* p. 134. Italics in text.)

This view is laid down by Marcuse in his usual confident style, and without qualification. But is it self-evident? It is a view that happens to be shared by a large number of men, particularly academics. But it is nevertheless erroneous. Let us consider the matter. The view holds for the kind of thinking engaged in by those who seek knowledge, whether theoretical or practical—knowledge that finds embodiment in language, in propositions tied together logically and leading in some order from assumptions to conclusions. But if the only genuine or authentic thought is abstract thought, one could not call "thought" much that goes on in our heads, if I may put it this way.

Take, as an important modality of thinking, what Lévi-Strauss, in the first chapter of *The Savage Mind,* calls "The Science of the Concrete." The concrete thinker selects, but he does not select quite as much of what is before him, and he selects differently from the abstract philosopher or physicist. He stays close to the things he is thinking about, which is why Lévi-Strauss speaks of his thinking as "concrete." If he did not select or abstract by means of his own categories and in terms of his practical goals and purposes, we could not say of him that he thought at all, but if he did not stay as close as he does to the problem at hand, he would not think concretely. This is no doubt hard on philosophers. But it is the case. Marcuse would have it that all thought is abstract, thus accomplishing three things: By the statement he erases the important differences between abstract and concrete thought, puts the way he thinks in a superior place, and denies those who do not think as he does the title of thinkers.

168

But more importantly, if the only genuine thought there is is abstract thought, Marcuse would have to show that in the composition of one of his symphonies Beethoven either first thought abstractly, like a philosopher or mathematician, and then translated his thought into music, or that he did not think at all. He would have to show the same method for Titian and Cézanne. This is the way some critics believe that novelists compose. They never heard, or never took seriously, what T. S. Eliot said of Henry James, that he had a mind so fine that no idea could violate it. A genuine composer or painter thinks, but he thinks in terms of his medium, or by means of it: a dancer thinks with her body in motion, although actually she does not have to move visibly in order to think with her body in motion. To that body, if she is a good dancer, is attached a head—often quite a voluminous head, so to speak. When a novelist first thinks out a situation or conflict in abstract terms and then seeks to dramatize it, you can be sure he is no storyteller, no yarnspinner. What is more, the true storyteller cannot always control, from the top of his head, what his characters will do. I read somewhere, quite some time ago, that Arnold Bennett said he was not one to let his characters take the whiphand over him. The only comment that can be made about this statement is that this is one of the reasons Arnold Bennett was Arnold Bennett, and not George Eliot. For we know about her that at times her characters had, so to speak, a will of their own, and went where they wanted to and not where she wanted them to go.

But this matter cannot be compressed into a simple rule. I have known painters who in words were totally inarticulate, but when they stood before the canvas were capable of prodigious and vital expression. And there are those who can use their eyes and hands and also their tongues—so to speak. Delacroix, for instance. Van Gogh was a great painter, but he was also a great letter writer, as a casual look will disclose. On Marcuse's view the activities of novelists, composers, dancers, goldsmiths, and all other kinds of artists, no less than Lévi-Strauss' concrete thinkers, could not be called "genuine thinking." But music critics speak of "musical ideas," and when they do they are not talking analogically, for a musical idea can be defined in musical terms, without recourse to comparisons to the ideas of philosophers. But ultimately, whether you call the work that Beethoven and Mozart, Titian and Pavlova did, "genuine" or "authentic" "thought" or not, one thing cannot be denied, and that is that a good deal of what they did was done "with their heads." There is more to the matter, for we do not find great difficulty in saying of a musical composition or a canvas that it is more profound than another. We may not be able to give an extended account of what we mean, but the felt quality of the distinction is there, for us, in the contrast between one work and the other.

Why do I make so much of a minor point, made almost by the way, by Marcuse, in *One-Dimensional Man?* The reason is that below I am going at greater length into the judgment I passed above when I said that Marcuse's recent thought was of the same quality as that of Wright Mills. His asseveration about genuine thought is part of the evidence.

IN ONE OF MARCUSE'S RECENT ESSAYS, ALREADY MEN-
tioned, "Repressive Tolerance," he expatiates and makes his
own the idea of tolerance that in *Reason and Revolution* he
attributed to the *philosophes.* In the latter he tells us that

> The French Enlighteners who fought the absolute state gave
> no relativist framework to their demand for tolerance, but as-
> serted that demand as part of their general effort to establish
> a better form of government . . . Tolerance did not mean jus-
> tice to all existing parties. It meant, in fact, the abolition of
> one of the most influential of parties, that of the clergy allied
> with the feudal nobility, which was using intolerance as an
> instrument for domination. (p. 355)

In the essay on "Repressive Tolerance" he expounds this very conception of tolerance on his own authority, thus appearing quite clearly for what all along we had known him to be, a Torquemada of the left. The essay claims to be an examination of the idea of tolerance in our advanced industrial society. And the conclusion, stated baldly in the second sentence of the first paragraph of the essay, is that

> the realization of the objective of tolerance would call for intolerance toward prevailing policies, attitudes, opinions, and the extension of tolerance to policies, attitudes, and opinions which are outlawed or suppressed.

Marcuse means exactly what he says. Tolerance for the negative thinker and his followers, the wreckers, equipped with minds that work with the delicacy of a sledgehammer. And those who do not agree? *Al paredón,* of course. For what can one do with agents of tyranny, obstructing stubbornly the creation of a world in which fear and pain will be abolished, labor will be done away with, and men will become polymorphously resexualized? These obstructionists are enemies of humanity. Take this loony sentence, and after you read it once, savor its fragrance of love of freedom: "The tolerance which enlarged the range and content of freedom was always partisan—intolerant towards the protagonists of the repressive status quo." No quarter should be given to the opposition.

Note that this is the considered program of a man who fights under the banner of "reason," a program labeled by the pretty name of "liberating tolerance." And what does it liberate you from, if you have the foolhardiness to disagree? When you are put up against a *paredón* you are entirely liberated, liberated from further pain, anxiety, disagreement with the truth, from further labor; in short, you are liberated from your life. This is the wisdom, dear reader, of a man who accuses our society of "reviving the brutality of medieval and early modern practices." It is we, who dare to disagree with Marcuse's "liberating tolerance," who are brutal.

The tolerance Marcuse denies is tolerance for a society that is a going affair, and the tolerance he favors is the nihilistic

172

tolerance for a society that he himself tells us not even he can conceive. For what else does the following sentence mean? "For the true positive is the society of the future and therefore beyond definition and determination, while the existing positive is that which must be surmounted." (*C P T,* p. 87) Has anyone ever run across someone else who embodies the overbearing dogmatism and the arrogant presumptuousness of this man? Bear clearly in mind, this is a man who asks us to destroy our society on his word, on his verbal assurance that while he cannot tell us what he is going to build when he razes all our institutions, we must give him a blank check, duly signed by all of us, to wreak his poisonous hatred on us.

Marcuse is probably not aware of the foul smell of hatred and bigotry, the daemonic megalomania, that steams from the pages of his essay on the advisability of the use of intolerance by those who wish to "liberate" mankind. These pages are among the ugliest, morally speaking, that he has written to date.

Since Marcuse has not yet enjoyed political power we have not yet had, thank Heaven, the opportunity of seeing him put into practice his generous notion of liberating tolerance. So far, he has had to be content with exercising liberating tolerance in a theoretical way only. But in so doing he has given evidence of high talent. Mention to him what we may take to be a positive virtue of our society. Without any effort whatever he shows it for what it is, a foul vice. Take, for instance, his treatment of the tolerance of an affluent democracy. He tells us that in such a society all points of view are tolerated. "Moreover," he adds,

in endlessly dragging debates over the media the stupid opinion is treated with the same respect as the intelligent one, the misinformed may talk as long as the informed, and propaganda rides along with education, truth with falsehood. This pure toleration of sense and nonsense is justified by the democratic argument that nobody, neither group nor individual, is in possession of the truth and capable of defining what is right and wrong, good and bad. (*C P T,* p. 94)

173

The Nazi mind sooner or later gives itself away. Call it elitism, the aristocracy of the mind, the true knowledge of the knowers, the superiority in virtue and knowledge of the guardians, the Nazi mind sooner or later discloses its contempt for what it deems the "stupid opinion" or the worthlessness of mass man. Marcuse is overwhelmed with concern for the repression under which mankind is suffering. But his is a fake concern; the hatred of domination is the sour-grapes attitude of a man who cannot put his hands at the controls.

But is it true that the toleration practiced by our affluent democracy is justified in the belief that no one knows the truth, the right, and the good? Of course it isn't. This is not even a caricature of the justification of our tolerance. But first let me set the record straight. What there is of actual tolerance in our society is not the monopoly of any one group, and least of all of liberals who should give the example of possessing it by living up to their principles. Indeed one could claim without too much exaggeration that Marcuse's principle of repressive tolerance, although not proclaimed, is one of the basic and most successfully operative principles that actually govern our world. In the academic world—about which I can speak with a modicum of authority—we welcome and honor intellectual termites of the Left, but men of the Right are loathed. They are ostracized. I know.

But what justifies the principle, if not the actuality, of tolerance? It is justified on the belief 1) that no one has the whole of the truth, and 2) that in the argument that takes place in freedom between the possessors of conflicting views that claim to be true, a better formulation can come about than was obtainable before, and even altogether new formulations of new truths may emerge, through the stimulation of one mind by another. People who use the term "think tanks" and other expressions of that sort use babbitt language. But the idea behind the language is not altogether false: In open discussion, in the stimulation that results from open debate, there can emerge new and valuable thought, and sometimes does.

I did not say that new and valuable thought always emerges. All one can claim is that the possibility is open, which without tolerance would never emerge. This is quite different from the perverse formulation we find in Marcuse's essay. But if nothing emerges and every participant in the debate goes home tired, frustrated, and utterly unconvinced by his opponents, something valuable accrues nevertheless. The man who listens knows better than he did before what others who oppose him want and why. And the possibility arises of a compromise, of the suggestion of a *modus vivendi.* And this, though far from ideal, is nevertheless much better than wars of religion or civil war or the intolerance advocated by Marcuse. Let me emphasize it: it is considerably better than having an arrogant Negative Guru dictate to us his Apodictic Truth.

Just in case some of my readers remain incredulous about my account of Marcuse's doctrine of intolerance, let me quote a statement in which he leaves us with no doubt about what he means:

> Liberating tolerance, then, would mean intolerance against movements from the Right, and toleration of movements from the Left. As to the scope of this tolerance and intolerance: . . . it would extend to the stage of action as well as of discussion and propaganda, of deed as well as of word. (*C P T,* p. 109)

True toleration is the toleration of the Left but not of those that oppose the Left. It is, in other words, the toleration of those we need not tolerate because they already agree with us, along general lines at least; but those that might demand toleration, because they do not agree with us, we ought not to tolerate. The power of words is greater, I suggest, than the power of negative thought, an insight we dimly had before Orwell brought it to full clarity. Notice further that there is nothing academic about Marcuse's toleration. He advises—for that is what it is, advice—repressive tolerance towards those who oppose him in action and deed. Remember what action and deed mean to a revolutionist. It does not mean discussion and propaganda, which he clearly contrasts with action and deed. It means the destruction of our world. There recently appeared a strangely ambivalent book on Marcuse, written by

175

Robert W. Marks, in which our negative thinker's program is respectably *endimanché* in attire fit for middle-class progressives, and is summed up in five theses that no one who accepts the secular ideology could possibly object to, for it adds up to the most reasonable of all worldly desiderata (*The Meaning of Marcuse,* New York, 1969). Marks quotes Marcuse (p. 93) as saying that the press has identified him with the student revolts, but actually he is opposed to campus violence. I remember having read an interview in which he said that he does not believe that books or paintings should be burnt. And he has also said that he does not want our modern industrial technology destroyed. Apparently he believes that action and deed can be carried on within controlled limits. Action and deed will only destroy men of the Right and the state, but not the museums and libraries; it will take over the factories without damaging them. This means that violent action—whether riots or the storming of the Bastille or of the Winter Palace—is to be carried on—but how far? When will the mob stop? Who will stop it? Intolerance, we are to believe, will be extended to the stage of action and deed. I must leave it to the reader to make up his mind about the clarity and the coherence of our negative thinker.

So deep is Marcuse's hatred, so narrow the focusing of his intelligence on what he takes to be our repressive society, that he does not see that his words disprove his own indictment. He writes:

> But with the concentration of economic and political power and the integration of opposites in a society which uses technology as an instrument of domination, effective dissent is blocked where it could freely emerge: in the formation of opinion, in information and communication, in speech and assembly. (*C P T,* p. 95)

Of this we can only ask when, where, and by what official agency, under what circumstances, has Marcuse been prevented from disseminating his hatred? Let me emphasize the official agency, because the threat on his life we cannot count, since it is not known whether the act was a joke or a seriously planned action by some group of extremists of the Right or of the Left. Or of the Left, let me emphasize, for when this book was in the process of final revision I came across further evidence of the hatred that the Russians have for him. See the article by B. Bykhovskiim in Vol. XXX, No. 2, December 1969, of *Philosophy and Phenomenological Research.*

As the essay was going through its final revision I also had before me a book entitled *The New Left, A Collection of Essays.* It is a hefty volume of 475 pages, containing twenty-eight different essays and a bibliography. The essays express, often coarsely, never irenically, never objectively, "effective dissent." The editors have not been jailed for publishing what in parts is simply libelous of the country and its system. Or does Marcuse define "effective dissent" so as to deny it to anyone who publishes the hatred these essays express?

19

THE NEXT SUBJECT REQUIRES EXTENDED TREATMENT. REA-
son plays a dominant role in Marcuse's thought. It is by an
appeal to reason that he condemns our society. And he gives
the impression that he knows himself to be in possession of a
corner on it and that disagreement with him is *eo ipso* a sort
of willful acceptance of error. One would expect that such a
man would have kept himself *au courant* of developments that
in our day have forced a serious modification of the classical
concept of reason. But such is not the case. In respect to the
concept of reason he is stuck in the past. The reason to which
he appeals is the classical notion of reason, inherited by the
great rationalists of the Seventeenth Century from Greco-
Roman and medieval thought, developed by these philosophers in the light of the new science, especially mathematics,

178

and employed by the *philosophes* in the Eighteenth Century.

It is of course widely known that Marcuse studied Hegel— he wrote a book subtitled "Hegel and The Rise of Social Theory." We have seen that he studied Husserl. But currents of thought that call for a modification of the classical concept of reason, although he is acquainted with them, have not influenced his understanding of it. One does not expect him to be sympathetic to Kierkegaard, but in *Reason and Revolution* there is evidence that he has read him. He is acquainted with Dostoevsky. He is, of course, acquainted with Nietzsche, and one of his sympathetic critics, Robinson, tells us that he "read extensively in Freud during the late 1930's." That in a sense he knows Freud it would be foolish to deny. We have already seen that he wrote a book in which he tries to avoid the Founder's pessimistic conceptions of human destiny. I shall show in this discussion that Marcuse does not know Freud well enough. But Marcuse has not responded to the challenge that these thinkers represent to the rationalists of the Seventeenth Century and their heirs in the Eighteenth and Nineteenth centuries, and in ours. In respect to the meaning—to the nature, the function, and the manner of operation—of the faculty of reason, Marcuse is, as I shall show in the following pages, decidedly old-fashioned. His concept of reason is obsolete.

In order to exhibit the defects of Marcuse's notion of reason I shall first turn to his own exposition of the meaning of the term, as used by the Eighteenth Century *philosophes*. (*R & R*, pp. 253-257) I cannot here summarize this discussion in its entirety. It is fairly concentrated already in the less than five pages in which it is presented and it does not lend itself to further condensation; but more to the point, not all he has to say about the idea of reason as conceived by the *philosophes* is relevant to my purposes. It will be sufficient to select from Marcuse's presentation those aspects of the old notion that are accepted by him. It is my claim that the aspects of the old notion that I shall select constitute the heart of Marcuse's own concept of reason and the way it functions. After showing that Marcuse's own conception of reason is congruous with that of the *philosophes,* I shall call attention to its defects.

179

Marcuse tells us that the concept of reason includes the belief that society is open to reform or to thorough reconstruction; this belief is the result of knowledge that a regnant scheme of things does not fulfill the desires of all those who are part of it. That the desires of all those who are part of a society should be fulfilled is apparently a proposition that is taken to be self-evident. It is also stated without qualification. But let that go. A social organization that fails to satisfy human desires is iniquitous. As society becomes more rational—as it learns more about its desires and the failure of the system to satisfy them—man's thought becomes autonomous. But the benefits of this autonomy are shared by everybody, for reason is universal. This means that reason considers the claims of all citizens of a commonwealth, taking "all" distributively, the claims of each and every one of them. Reason, then, is the means through which men discover the universal potentialities that claim realization. The conception of reason involves, further, the idea of freedom. But here a complication sets in; for the pattern of successful thought is that employed by natural science. It follows that the human world is taken to be governed by objective laws, "analogous or even identical with the laws of nature." On such a view, freedom can only mean man's efforts to adapt himself to necessity that is analogous or identical with physical law. Because of this analogy or identity I submit that the following formulation of this view is not a travesty: Man's perfect freedom consists of being a perfect slave to the nature of things. Control means submission.

One aspect of this conception of reason calls for emphatic iteration because it is obviously of paramount importance for our purposes: The world, the non-human and the human worlds, can be understood and changed by man's knowledge and action. In the light of our critical knowledge no extant arrangements, no institutions of any kind, however old, can claim to be above the reach of criticism and alteration. If need be, institutions and the whole of society must be destroyed and rebuilt. In my own blunt terms: The past has no claim on the present, nor has the present any guaranteed stability, unless a society's institutions can "deliver"; and what social institutions

180

are called on to deliver is the satisfactions of the worldly desires of all men, of each and every one. If it cannot deliver, that society stands condemned and ought to be reformed or destroyed.

We turn to Marcuse's own notion of reason. He gives us a view of it in passing in the first essay in *Negations*, "The Struggle Against Liberalism In the Totalitarian View of The State." Many other references to reason are to be found in his writings. Unfortunately we do not find, in the readily available texts, a fully developed account of what he takes the term to mean. From the contrast drawn by Marcuse between the liberal view of society and the totalitarian or Nazi view, I believe we are free to gather that Marcuse accepts the former as far as it goes. He finds it rational as against the irrational concept of the state of the Nazis. It almost goes without saying that for Marcuse the liberal view of the state is defective. Why? For reasons he adduces, which need not be reviewed here, and that add up to the fact that the liberal state contains the seed of the totalitarian state, into which it finally turns.

I shall follow, almost *au pied de la lettre,* Marcuse's exposition of the rational theory of society. A theory of society is rational when it acknowledges the autonomy of reason, by which is understood "the human faculty of comprehending, through conceptual thought, the true, the good, and the right." (*N,* p. 14) The legitimation of action and of goals within the society, and the legitimation of society itself, is achieved by the judgment of reason. Nothing falls out of its jurisdiction, neither fact nor goal. A connection is said to be rational when it meets the exigencies of the principle of sufficient reason. One reader at least would like to know more about the principle than Marcuse gives us, particularly he would like to know why does Marcuse restrict the principle in a way Leibniz would have found narrowing and impoverishing.

We are told, further, that the mere existence of facts or goals does not require us to acknowledge them; acknowledgement, Marcuse adds, "occurs" when knowledge has decided that the fact or goal is in accordance with reason. Marcuse must be using the verb "to acknowledge," and related terms, in a pri-

181

vate sense. Interpreted literally, the statement is nonsense. The facts and goals of Nazi Germany had, and still have, to be acknowledged. They were acknowledged by one of its victims who escaped to Switzerland and finally landed in New York, to become a powerful hater of American society. They were acknowledged by the millions who could not escape the butchers. They were finally acknowledged by Chamberlain in spite of his struthonian compulsion. And they are acknowledged today by historians. Marcuse probably means by this outlandish statement that facts and goals ought not to be approved or accepted as legitimate or taken as acceptable unless they pass rational muster. Otherwise they must be condemned. But he does not say this. I make a point of a matter that is relatively trivial because it shows again how careless Marcuse is in the expression of his thought.

At this point in Marcuse's exposition of the rationalist theory of society an important component is introduced. I shall quote a long passage, because I am not certain that I can transliterate Marcuse into English. We are told that:

> The rationalist theory of society is therefore essentially *critical;* it subjects society to the idea of a theoretical and practical, positive and negative critique. This critique has two guidelines: first, the given situation of man as a rational organism, i. e., one that has the potentiality of freely determining and shaping his own existence, directed by the process of knowledge and with regard to his worldly happiness; second, the given level of development of the productive forces and the (corresponding or conflicting) relations of production as the criterion for those potentialities that can be realized at any given time in men's rational structuring of society. The rationalist theory is well aware of the limits of human knowledge and of rational social action, but it avoids fixing these limits too hurriedly and, above all, making capital out of them for the purpose of uncritically sanctioning established hierarchies. (*N*, p. 15)

One reader, at least, cannot be confident that he understands this passage. The second "guideline" is stated in a sentence that one has to squeeze into grammatical form by force,

182

for as it is written it does not parse readily. The three "givens" do not make that which follows them specific; on a hunch, one decides that the explanatory sentence that follows the *id est* does not refer to the whole sentence that precedes the *id est,* as one would expect it to, but solely to "rational organism," whose meaning it unfolds. When one has puzzled the quotation out, what Marcuse seems to mean is this: A rationalist theory of society is critical and criticizes society both theoretically and practically, positively and negatively. The criticism is carried on by means of two guidelines. One of them is the tenet that man is a rational being, that is, that he is capable of determining and shaping his own existence. The activity of determining and shaping human existence is carried on with the help of knowledge and is addressed to the securing of worldly happiness. The other guideline is this: To undertake the criticism of society, the critic attains to the level of development of the productive forces and the (corresponding or conflicting) relations of production. These relations constitute a criterion that enables the critic to decide what potentialities can be realized in order to reform or transform society according to a rational plan. I am puzzled by "the (corresponding and conflicting) relations of production," because it is not clear why "corresponding and conflicting" are enclosed in parentheses; I am also puzzled by what is intended by the term "the relations of production." Relations of what kind? Relations between or among what terms? Again, does the "or" indicate an antithesis or a disjunction between "corresponding" and "conflicting"? If these terms are antithetical, "corresponding" would seem to mean "in harmony." If the "or" is not used antithetically but to convey a simple disjunction, the statement is not intelligible, for two processes may correspond to something, to anything, and because they are not antithetical they may overlap. Thus the passage quoted must be interpreted by fiat. One's reading of it may or may not be congruous with Marcuse's meaning. The last sentence presents no difficulty.

We have enough before us to draw a comparison between Marcuse's understanding of the classical notion of reason and his own in order to comment on the latter. But note that, with

183

one exception, it will not be a question of the correctness of Marcuse's understanding of the concept of reason accepted by the middle class as an ideological weapon. The question we are interested in, here, is the extent to which Marcuse's own concept of reason is similar to, or the same as, the classical concept. And the answer to the question is that in their important components the concepts are identical. He claims autonomy for the classical notion and for his own; for each he claims critical primacy; for each he also claims universality and freedom; and for each he claims that, working autonomously, reason addresses itself to the task of so reshaping society as to secure for all men, for each and every one, worldly happiness by satisfying their desires.

Before I go on to the examination of Marcuse's own concept of reason, in fairness to myself I must be permitted to make the following declaration. I want to make this declaration as emphatically, as categorically, and as clearly as I can make it: To point out that some of the criticisms leveled by the Nazis at a liberal theory of society are right or valid, or admissible, is not to argue that the Nazi ideology or philosophy they would put in place of liberal ideology or philosophy is right, or valid, or admissible. The Nazis could have been to some extent, or even entirely, right about liberal social theory, right about what they rejected, and could have been wrong, as indeed they were, about what they accepted. It could also be possible that some of the formulations of their own theory and of their criticisms of liberal theory were not the best they could have arrived at.

Let me begin my examination of Marcuse's own concept of reason by considering a criticism he makes of the Nazi theory of society. He holds that it is irrational. But first of all, a purely terminological question. The distinction between society and the state is of the greatest importance for some purposes. But it will be neglected here, particularly when we are considering Nazi theory, since it claimed that the Nazi state—the institutions and instrumentalities by which the German people were governed in Hitler's day—and the people or folk, were one. It also claimed that the folk's intentions were perfectly expressed by their leader.

One of the criticisms made by the Nazis of the liberal theory of the state was that it was "rootless." Marcuse takes up this criticism, but instead of showing that his view of the liberal state is not rootless, he argues against the Nazi notion of "rootedness" as follows: By rooting their theory, the Nazis make it irrational. They place irrational "givens," or "pregiven facts" prior to the autonomy of reason and thus limit that autonomy. (Let me say in passing that I shall use the terms used by Marcuse, although the reader will find them as aesthetically offensive as I do. I use them because I doubt whether we could substitute "a priori" for "pregiven".) This "functionalizes" reason and annihilates its force and effectiveness, because it turns the irrational pregivens into normative principles. And this robs reason of its autonomy by placing it under the heteronomy of the irrational. Marcuse argues, further, that to root reason is to justify a society by submerging in the hidden darkness of "blood" or of "the soul" contradictions that conceptual knowledge recognizes.

A question we must ask of Marcuse's criticism of Nazi theory is this: Why is it wrong for the Nazis to "functionalize" reason, when Marcuse does not object to the middle class "functionalizing" it? As we shall see below, Marcuse tells us that for the middle class reason was a "slogan." (R R, p. 253) I do not know the answer to this question, unless the answer is that we have here an early deduction from a principle he develops quite explicitly much later in his notorious essay "Repressive Tolerance." According to this principle, what is wrong for Marcuse's enemies is not wrong for his friends—even if the acts performed and the judgments enunciated by both sides are performed or enunciated under similar circumstances.

Let us ask what can be said about the Nazi criticism of Marcuse's interpretation of the liberal theory of society. We can say with confidence that it is wrong. But it must also be said that the liberal theory defended by Marcuse is wrong. What the Nazis should have said was that the theory of liberal society was rooted in ground that the national socialists did not accept as valid ground. Marcuse, however, seems to believe that the liberal theory was derived from autonomous reason itself and that it eschews all pregivens that threaten the primacy of reason. But this claim is merely laid down; he never validates it, nor could he validate it were he to try to do so. In fact he posits "worldly happiness" as a pre-given, or at any rate as a demand about which there can be no argument, in the very way in which "blood," and the "folk," and the leader are posited by the Nazis. And this is rooting, or tantamount to rooting, his view of the state in a conception of man and his destiny. Logically, then, both theories are rooted. That the Nazis do not accept as valid the ground in which liberalism is rooted, does not mean that it is not rooted there. And that Marcuse seems to agree with the Nazis that liberalism is not encumbered by pregivens does not mean that his conception of liberal theory lacks pregivens. What then is the difference between one theory and the other? None whatever in respect to the condition of being rooted, for both are. This can be restated as follows: In the order of logic there is no difference whatever between these two theories. The difference between them is substantive. They aim at the realization of different social and political systems.

What more can be said about Marcuse's concept of reason? Observe, first, that reason is not a thing, and neither is the mind a thing. In discussing the classical notion, Marcuse calls reason, at least once, "a faculty," this is to say a power, an ability. But in the usual employment of the term he conveys the impression that for him reason is indeed a thing, that it has ontic status rather than being functional. Reason on this view is of the nature of being itself and therefore there are acts, judgments, customs, practices and institutions that go counter to its grain. But this notion of reason is a version of the classical notion to which the scientists of the Seventeenth Century sang paeans, as when men like Galileo and Huygens exclaimed that Geometry was the alphabet of God. This notion can deliver substantive judgments, for it is an expression of the real, which is, itself, value freighted. But if reason is not a thing but a faculty, a way of minding, if reason is reasoning, it has no other role than the control and criticism of the way in which propositions are illated. On this view we can still speak of an irrational action or an irrational institution, but the irrationality of the action or the institution arises from the fact that it goes against a value premise that is assumed to control normatively a set of practices, or social arrangements, or decisions. Thus sexual repression is said to be irrational by a hedonist because he believes that the fulfillment of desire is good or a good. And for the Marxist, religion is irrational because he takes it to be a human device to keep man happy in his chains. It is not superfluous to note that the ontic conception of reason is a close relative of the notion of natural law defended by classical philosophers and still believed in by orthodox theists and many conservative thinkers and scholars. That such notions as an ontic reason and the idea of natural law are obsolete, is something which I cannot stop to discuss here. Against the classical theory of natural law I have written elsewhere.

Reason, then, is reasoning, a way of minding—indeed the only admissible way of minding for conceptual thought. One's minding is rational when it follows the rules of good reasoning. When one's minding is rational, it works on the matter of experience, and that matter is as varied as the multiplicity of objects of human interest. Reason, which is to say, reasoning, can be employed at any task. The Nazis employed it in the devising of means for murdering millions of people as efficiently as possible. And Stalin employed it in the years of terror to do away with, it has been calculated, ten to twelve million Russians. Reasoning is not pledged to advance causes that we call good and put obstacles to the realization of causes we call evil. When we say "war is irrational" we mean that it is contrary to a concept of the good life. But this concept cannot be educed, or derived, or somehow squeezed from the notion of reason by itself.

Note that all of the problems that arise when we reason about reason, urgent as they are—the vast, complex, the puzzling problem of mind, its nature, its ways of achieving good results, the relation of mind to physiology and of reason to morality and many more problems—are open problems. They can only be closed by faith, dogmatism, or ignorance. No one has the infallible, the apodictic answer to any one of them. But that does not mean that we are not entitled to hold with a modicum of diffident confidence some tenets. I hold two with some confidence: One is that reason is reasoning and mind is minding. The other is that each one of us owes each one of the others respect, regardless of who he is or what he is. This, I believe, is the basis of morality, and it is because it is not observed that the world we live in, the world man has always lived in, is and has always been a stinking chaos. How to make these two tenets go together is a difficult problem: fortunately it is not one we need to consider here. But I would like to iterate that all these questions are open questions.

Insofar as these observations are correct, Marcuse's concept of reason is defective. But it is also crippled by other defects, to the consideration of which I invite the reader. The first is Marcuse's failure to notice the important difference between his own interpretation of the classical concept of reason and the understanding of it that the philosophers of the Seventeenth Century and later, the *philosophes,* had. He writes:

> Beginning with the Seventeenth Century, philosophy had quite definitely absorbed the principles of the rising middle class. Reason was the critical slogan of this class, with which it fought all who hampered its political and economic development. The term saw service in the war of science and philosophy against the Church, in the attack of the French enlightenment on absolutism, and in the debate between liberalism and mercantilism. . . Its meaning changed with the changing position of the middle class. (*R R,* p. 253)

In this passage we find Marcuse again overriding important differences in favor of a thesis. Some of the principles and doctrines advanced by Seventeenth-Century rationalists were no doubt useful to the middle class in its struggle against the *ancien régime.* But that all the great Seventeenth Century

188

philosophers aided the middle class is simply not true. Consider: Marcuse mentions Descartes, Hobbes, Spinoza and Leibniz by name. First, these men did not think of themselves as propagandists or ideologues—if I may be permitted the anachronistic terminology. They were elaborating systems they took to be true. But above all, they were not serving the same ends. Descartes seemed to some of his contemporaries to be a destructive force. But he was soon appreciated for what he truly was, a man bent on conserving the ancient values while making room for the new science. The Jesuits, a powerfully progressive force in some respects at some times in some places, taught Descartes in Mexico in the early Eighteenth Century. From the beginning Hobbes was feared as subversive, and the whole effort of the British moralists who followed him may be said to have been put into repairing the intellectual damage he was responsible for. But the fact that he encountered strong opposition indicates that Seventeenth-Century philosophy was not employed solely in one single task. Spinoza, known to a very small number of *savants* during his lifetime, was indeed a subversive force, both religiously and socio-politically. But his influence was not felt in the Seventeenth Century. He was virtually unknown for about a hundred years more or less after his death. And Leibniz, who in some respects was a bold intellectual adventurer—as well as, perhaps, the last of the genuine polymaths—exercised a powerful conservative influence in other respects. His monadology could be interpreted as encouraging individualism of an extreme kind. His discoveries in mathematics and semiosis were profoundly innovative. But their influence was not felt immediately outside the field of pure knowledge. And his theodicy and his efforts in favor of teleology were plainly conservative.

There is more: What Marcuse tells us about the relationship between reason and class interest is not clear. He tells us that philosophy "absorbed" the principles of the middle class. But who in the middle class first formulated these principles for the philosophers to absorb them? *Pace* Marcuse's Marxist sociology of knowledge, it is very likely that it was the philosophers who first formulated the principles they advocated, by which the middle class sought to carry on its struggle against the *ancien régime*. If the philosophers had found them already made and merely absorbed them, what use could the middle class have had for philosophers? One can go on asking questions that expose the muddle of the passage quoted: but the problem gets more difficult the further one penetrates into the Marcusean bog. Enough to say that if philosophy absorbs its principles from the middle or any other class, we have the problem of explaining exactly in what sense it can be said that philosophy is both autonomous and the servant of the middle class. To say that a term saw service in a war is to borrow a locution from military parlance. A certain man saw service in the Crimea; another in the Pacific in the war against Japan. They could be meritorious heroes or contemptible cowards; in respect to their service they may have been "true" or "false," not in an epistemological sense but in the moral sense of these terms. We are also told that the meaning of "reason" changed with the changing position of the middle class. But the important question, left unanswered, is what initiated the change, what controlled its direction, what goal or goals were the changes devised to achieve. If the changes were the result of epistemological inquiries, whatever factors suggested the inquiries, these factors need not have affected the result of inquiry. And whatever the results of epistemological inquiries, the use to which they may have been put is irrelevant to the validity or adequacy of the new meaning of the term "reason." If the meaning of the term "reason" was given it by epistemological, psychological and, in general, philosophical inquiry, the use to which the term was put does not affect the autonomy that it has been discovered to have.

Marcuse holds that reason is a weapon with which the middle class fought for its interests. And clearly it is by an appeal to reason that he fights the Nazis who once threatened his Marxist-Freudian dystopia. Does he hold that reason is only a weapon? He does not state what else he takes it to be. But if reason is only a weapon, why should it command respect either from those not engaged in the fight or from those on the opposite side of it? A mind that values its autarchy need not respect

190

useless weapons, and those it respects, it respects as weapons, not as truths.

In fact it is hard to believe that for Marcuse reason is only a weapon. It was indeed used as a slogan, but it must have been taken to be more than a slogan by those who used it against the *ancien régime* or it would have been useless to them; and I hope it is taken to be more than a slogan by Marcuse or we shall have to say that he is far more in error than he is. But however Marcuse takes it, we know that those who used it against the *ancien régime* used it because they were confident that they had a hold of the truth and their enemies had nothing but superstition on their side.

THREE OTHER CRITICISMS OF MARCUSE'S CONCEPT OF
reason must be put on record. The first is that his understanding of the nature of reason has remained pre-Freudian. Let us
see why.

As already noted, the matter of experience offered to reason
for elaboration—for elucidation and ordering—is value-
freighted. But values do not exercise their requiredness on a
mirror mind. The mind to which they present themselves as
valuable is constitutive, and its constitutive power depends not
merely on categorial schemes that are open for criticism at the
conscious level, but on factors of selection and rejection that
work below the level of awareness. The objective and the subjective landscapes present themselves to a mind as having the
characters they have, not merely because they are what they
are, but because the particular mind to which they present

themselves is what it is. We can check the premises of our reasoning—to some extent. What are ordinarily called "facts" are brute facts as regards which there ought not to be disagreement. But the values the facts are freighted with give rise to questions about which agreement is considerably more difficult and often in fact—although never in theory—impossible. And the source of the difficulty or impossibility of deciding exactly whether a value that we have before us is indeed a value or a disvalue, and what place in the hierarchy it occupies, is that a man's apprehension of a value is not like his apprehension of a color or like his reading of the mercury column in a thermometer. The apprehension of values or disvalues depends much more than the apprehension of "mere facts" on unconscious drives and psychic formations the operation of which we can seldom be completely aware of. It cannot be fully clear to a man why he esteems another or detests him, or why he prefers one painting to another. Some reasons can be given and the process of validation can be carried out much farther than it is usually carried in the disorderly hurly-burly of social living. But some factors that contribute to the acceptance or rejection of value features of experience remain altogether hidden. Some of these remain forever, in fact, if not in principle, beyond exposure to the light of consciousness and criticism. Whether a man wants worldly happiness or self-destruction, and what specific content he gives to the notion of happiness, is a matter on which reason has indeed a say. But it does not have the sole say; other agencies have a say also. Habituation, psychological aptitudes and defects, trained perception of value along some lines and myopia along others, native sensibility cultivated or left to function in its uncultivated form, and many more such factors affect our apprehension of value or disvalue. One that is conspicuous by absence from awareness, but that exerts a powerful influence on our value predilections, is that component of the self that Freud called "a chaos, a cauldron full of seething excitations," the id.

These remarks do not put me on the side of the emotivists in ethics, for they hold that the emotive component of our valuations is, in principle, intractable to reason, is altogether

193

beyond the reach of rational suasion. The student of Freud cannot agree with this assumption. If value formations could not be reasoned with, in principle at least, psychoanalysis would be, in principle, impossible. Value conflicts can effectively be reasoned about, and in some cases, among some persons, about some subjects, it is possible to resolve value conflicts rationally, although it must be acknowledged that the rational resolution of value conflicts is a rare event in human experience.

It should be more or less evident that the acceptance of a pre-Freudian notion of mind enables Marcuse to put an unqualified faith in reason that a post-Freudian cannot put in it. For the latter, the scope of reason is limited and the limitations, varying from person to person, from culture to culture, and from subject matter to subject matter, are inherent in the development of the mind. This accounts for the troublesome fact that what seems to one person rational seems irrational to another. And also for the fact that conflict seems to be an endemic and pandemic condition of human life.

To point this out is not, of course, to proclaim the virtues of irrationality, or to side with the revolt against reason, or to appeal to the blood, or anything of the kind. It is one of the basic demands of reason, I would imagine, that we define as carefully as we can its limits and its limitations, its power and its weakness, that we do not put more weight on it than it is in its nature to carry. Philosophers who, today, speak of "Sovereign Reason" are petty despots in love with their rhetoric. Reason has limited jurisdiction and, if unqualified, its sovereignty is usurped. For men it is the energies of the body that have ultimate control. Let them fail and it is said that reason is washed up from three to five minutes after the heart ceases to pump. In our day a number of philosophers have warned against the contemporary revolt against reason. Collingwood, Morris Cohen, Brand Blanshard come readily to mind. Whether the revolt is peculiar to our age or constitutes one feature of the permanent revolution that is the process of human history, one reason for the anti-rationalism of our day, I suggest, is the failure on the part of the defenders of reason to

194

acknowledge the need to review its capacities in the light of recent findings about the mind.

The second criticism of Marcuse's concept of reason that must be put on record was touched on, in passing, above: the irrelevance, for his notion of it, of history in what he calls the "structuring" of society. I have already noted that Marcuse reiterates frequently that his critical analysis of society is "historical." But he does not mean that he has consulted archives, pondered over yellow documents, studied inscriptions and coins, or undertaken digs, or that he has read the works of men who have carried on these or similar activities. With the actual process of events, as reported by historians, he shows no central preoccupation. By history he means a philosophy of history, in terms of which he interprets the development of society. It enables him to tell *a priori* how events will occur. He tells us that criticism will not respect hierarchies; and he seems to hold that all that is needed to construct a good society is knowledge of man's needs and the reason to devise instrumentalities to satisfy these needs. It is not clear what the relation of the goal, the satisfaction of worldly desires, is to reason. He seems to believe, as I noted above, that the idea of worldly happiness can be educed from reason itself. But this is not at all clear, because his references to the role that reason plays in the construction or reconstruction of society are brief and assertoric. He does not take the trouble to explain why reason should prefer the goal of worldly happiness to any other goal man has pursued in history. In any case, wherever the goal comes from, and whatever legitimation it may be capable of, reason seeks to rear a society whose institutions are shaped to achieve it. But in the rearing of these institutions the past is not assigned a role. We are not told explicitly that reason has no use for the past. But in general the past has no authority for Marcuse. I can think off-hand of only two places in which he appeals to tradition. Criticizing the Nazis, he brings up against them that their conception of heroic realism "stands in sharp opposition to all the ideals acquired by Western man in the last centuries." (*N*, p. 30) The other place is in his recent presidential address

195

to the Pacific Division of the American Philosophical Association.

This statement may sound preposterous at first sight when directed against a man who refers frequently to history. But it is not preposterous. For Marcuse's frequent references to history are intended to emphasize the flux, and never its availability as a source of inspiration or wisdom. If Marcuse is aware of the powerful effect of the past on the present, it is to bewail it, to condemn its irrationality, to denounce its iniquities. For him the past is something to be surmounted, not to be wisely used. Reason attends to its crimes to do away with them and make certain that they will not be repeated.

The fact that a society is at any one time what it is by virtue of its history, that to a large extent the present is the product of the past and that the past is never fully past, never fully done away with, that to a greater or lesser extent it lives in the present and controls it, that by having been what it was, the past excludes certain possibilities and favors others, the fact that the sense of identity of a people, an essential component of its well-being, depends on the maintenance of the historical elements that are perhaps the most important constituents of that identity—none of these facts enters into his allegedly rational criticism of society.

It is this systematic oversight on his part that opens his views, as it opens the ideologies of perhaps all reformers and revolutionaries, to the criticism of the Nazis when they point out that the liberal theory of society is "rootless." The Nazis were right—as much as one may hate to admit that those monstrous butchers were ever right. I have already suggested that contemporary liberal and radical theory is essentially futuristic. Let me now suggest that this is an expression, in social and political thinking, of the evolutionist faith that pervades the modern mind. But whatever it is or wherever it comes from, it is there. The uselessness of the past is a deeply hidden assumption of the revolutionist, seldom stated, never examined irenically, always present, nevertheless, in his chiliastic dreams. In this respect Marcuse is a typical revolutionist.

The Nazis, of course, had the wrong symbols. Aside from the

fact that the notions of blood and race are taken by large numbers of people to be scientifically in disrepute, the fact ought to be self-evident that a highly technological, predominantly urban mass society, tending towards anonymity, cannot be based on these concepts. But at least the Nazis saw the need to root society in the traditions of its members.

I am not saying here that a thinker ought not to ignore tradition. I shall argue that below. Here I am merely pointing out that Marcuse ignores it. And I am also saying that traditions cannot be ignored. And they cannot be, because they are not easily uprooted, however hard a revolutionary regime may try to uproot them. One example of the fact is sufficient proof of the statement: the fate of religion in Russia; the way religion perdures in spite of the effort to do away with it. When traditions are ignored, they continue to be effective elements in the shaping of the quality of life of a society, but do so in secret, hence uncritically, and may therefore do harm.

Traditions are difficult to uproot because they are not only conveyed in the habits the child learns, in the rituals, ceremonies, and customary activities of a people, carried also in the physical equipment of a people, and carried in the *Weltanschauung,* but they are also carried by another medium, hardly tractable: the language of a society. Let us grant for the sake of the argument that all the carriers of tradition can be modified by political and legislative action. The language cannot be altered as easily as the others. Even if we do not appeal to Cassirer, or to the Sapir-Whorf hypothesis, it is still the case that the language of a people is one of the chief vessels of its traditions. The Americans tried to eradicate Spanish from the Philippines, and English is the language of the younger college generation today, I understand. But Spanish still lingers and Tagalog has not yet been eradicated. The Puerto Rican case, I believe, is somewhat similar.

But I also argue that could tradition be easily eradicated, it ought not to be. Not that it is sacred or untouchable. But that, aside from the fact that it contains precious wisdom that ought to be conserved, it is one of the sources of eliciting piety from normal human beings. And piety in man is essential to the

197

depth and richness of his life. A leftist literary critic has recently been quoted as writing that piety of whatever sort is alien to his temperament. One wonders what sort of a man he could be? A monster, of course. A charitable interpretation of this monstrous self-indictment is that the critic does not understand the meaning of the term "piety." Vulgarly, it is attached to objects of religious worship, and taken by village atheists, wherever they live, to have a slightly pejorative sense. It may have it even among believers. But in its original sense, in the Roman sense, it is a noble emotion, consisting of gratitude and reverence towards the sources of one's being. A man whose development has not been crippled, has piety towards his parents and his ancestry; towards his wife, when she is the source of profound well-being, as she can be; towards the "city" or nation, because the city or nation has made him what he is. He also has piety towards the cosmos, for to its mysterious creativity he traces ultimately the fact of his existence.

It is true that in the development of an individual many psychological factors enter that often impede the spontaneous response of gratitude and reverence towards the sources of one's being. It is also true that technology, as Ellul points out, desacralizes the world, and that contemporary philosophical naturalism—which is probably the *Weltanschauung* of the vast majority of educated men today—dries up the sense of piety a man may have towards the cosmos. It did not in Spinoza, who referred to it as "the intellectual love of God." It does in contemporary naturalists. But if men do not have piety towards the traditional objects—parents and ancestry, nation, cosmos—they soon find themselves responding with piety to objects that are not the proper stimuli of such emotion. In any case, a man really incapable of piety towards any object whatever is a monstrous individual, amoral, brutal, shallow, insensitive, and moved only by over-weening pride.

The third criticism to which Marcuse's notion of reason is open is that his understanding of human nature neglects an important component of the mind that Freud elucidated. We are told that rational society undertakes to satisfy the worldly desires of its members. When, in *Eros and Civilization,* Marcuse states that spiritual values are legitimate, he must mean what the Germans call the *geistig*, not the *geistlich*, desires of a man, the mental, not the spiritual. All that needs be said about his exclusion of spiritual desires is that this is to be expected of him.

However, belief that society can satisfy the desires of its members makes sense only on a pre-Freudian conception of the mind, according to which a man's desires or drives are available for direct inspection by turning attention inward, that they can easily be expressed in language, and that devices can be provided for their satisfaction. It is hardly necessary to mention that not all desires can be satisfied. What must be stated is that if all there was to the discovery of our desires was an act of introspection, the moral life would not be as difficult —not to say as hopeless—an undertaking as it is. A man who takes Freud seriously knows that the desires open for direct introspection are a very small part of the drives he harbors.

Let us consider the matter further. First, let us remember that Marcuse accepts Freud's "instinct" psychology— a psychology of drives, *Trieben*, factors that it is proper to call "instincts," because they are part of the organism's equipment prior to the modifications it receives from society. These instincts have their locus in the id, and seek satisfaction. Some of the drives can be satisfied indirectly, through sublimation, but others, it would seem, are permanently repressed for diverse reasons. The desire of the male infant for the mother is one of the drives that is condemned to permanent repression—unless it is dug out, so to speak, under therapeutic treatment. In the expression and repression of these instincts, two agencies are involved: the ego and the super-ego, which I shall on occasion, in the following pages, call the conscious self and the conscience.

It is Freud's basic assumption that the drives that seek expression are all of two kinds, the erotic drives and the self-destructive ones. Whether we accept this assumption or not— and I tend to reject it as too drastic a reduction—what we have learned from Freud is that in the deepest recesses of our personality, deep below consciousness, in the id, there is a psychic

199

content that has very tenuous and fortuitous connections with the external world. Those drives that manage to find satisfaction through sublimation never find adequate satisfaction. Nor is sublimation always possible. Hence the discontent to which we are condemned. Thus the conscious life of man, his public life, is a life carried on by a bio-psychic organism that is the victim of pressure both from his depths and from the environment. Adequate relief could come only from full satisfaction of all the drives that seethe in the caldron. This would not only be impossible—although not in the logical sense of "impossible"—for the individual in a private or idiotic sense—using the term etymologically—but it would be impossible for him socially. Impossible in the idiotic sense, because the satisfaction of some of his drives would prevent the satisfaction of other drives, since there is mutual incompatibility among them; and impossible in the social sense, because the collectivity, acting with regard to its own safety, simply cannot allow its members, taken distributively, to satisfy all their drives. There is enough chaos as it is in human society to imagine that much more is possible. Our public life—whether lived in solitude or in the company of our fellow beings—is ruled by social conventions, moral formulae, permissions and prohibitions, rituals and customs which taken together make up the quality of a group's experience, such as it is. Some of these rules, formulae, permissions and prohibitions are arbitrary; some seem to be but are not, because they contribute to the quality of the whole. When a form of life is instituted, it becomes valuable, even if it involves, as it always does, frustrations, irritation and pain. The justification, in any case for the rules and formulae that guide social life, is always public. And while I say this I am not forgetting that there are autarchs among us and probably in every society.

It is necessary to bear in mind that the content of the inaccessible regions of the id is in constant chaos, the war of all drives against all drives, all of them untamed, not all of them susceptible of taming by being objectified through sublimation, and being led to find more or less licit means of satisfaction. Consciousness and conscience reject their undisguised objectification and satisfaction, and try to keep them under a permanent ban; and the social ambient medium reinforces the introjected values the infant picked up that went into the formation of his super-ego.

It is this fact, this complex phenomenon about repression, sublimation and inadequate satisfaction, probably, that Freud in part included in his famous statement to the effect that the " 'ego' of each one of us . . . is not master in his own house, but . . . must be content with the veriest scraps of information about what is going on unconsciously in his own mind." The control by the vicar of society in the adult, the super-ego, and by the ego, seeks adaptation to the demands of society. But the outward pressure from the inaccessible depths engages in constant contravention of the public demands. Even in sleep the wild beasts underneath seek escape; and they find it then much more easily, as we know, than when we are awake and on our guard. Pressing out, inchoate demands force the guardians of the public in each of us to be on the alert—but through slips of the tongue, trivial mistakes, day-dreams of which we are barely conscious, and numerous other tricks, they get out, although they never enjoy in full their sojourn in the public world.

There are, of course, broad differences among human beings about the rigor with which the beasts caged in the id are kept down. The upright, rigorously repressed individual, a despot towards himself, keeps a better guard on the id than the relaxed, self-indulgent individual. And what is true of persons is true of cultures, and of different historical periods of a civilization. We have witnessed in the last three to five decades a relaxation of the public morality in the United States and, it seems, in the rest of the Western World, that was inconceivable immediately after the conclusion of the First World War. But the upright man—a reflexive despot, I shall call him—pays his price for his worship of morality. And the knowledgeable observer can discover in part the price the reflexive despot pays. His analyst, if he ever lands on a couch, finds that what his suave, neat, middle-class exterior covers is a sewer unspeakably stinking, in

201

which enormous voracious rats scurry, seeking exits.

Here, in the privacy or idiocy of a man, no less than in the society of which he is a member, we find the sources of the cruelty, the contempt, the scorn, the hardness, the indifference and the envy, the gratuitous malice towards oneself and towards others, that are the invariable components, to a greater or lesser extent, of the daily life of men in groups. This does not seem to be, it cannot be solely, a matter of the exploitation of the many by the few. Domination, exploitation cannot be denied. They exist in all societies, even in the smallest, the family. But human misery is not solely a matter of social domination. The systematic, deliberate use of men for alien purposes seems to be a feature of all societies. It may have reached one of its peaks in Rome, and another in the early decades of the industrial revolution. It is not to be condoned. But it is not the sole source of misery or pain, of frustration, of "discontent." It will be remembered that "domination" is not an ultimate term for Marcuse. In the beginning of history, domination was brought about, according to him, by scarcity. And it was kept up in society because scarcity has been a permanent feature of all societies—or nearly all, I would say. It is, therefore, scarcity that is the basic term. But in advanced industrial societies retention of domination is not fully explained by Marcuse. This, however, is a minor matter. The most serious defect of his analysis is that he finds that the whole of the individual's misery has its source in society.

But even if society were made up of saints, even if every one of its members were utterly selfless, unassertive, generous, charitable, good-hearted, sensitive towards others, free from malice and envy, and of course free from social domination, in such a utopia there would still be frustration for its members. For frustration is generated within each man because there are others next to him. Each man needs the rest of his fellow beings, but he finds them at the same time in his way. Even if each behaved in a saintly fashion towards each of the others they would still stand in his way.

But note that the standing in the way begins with oneself, and this is probably true of the most narcissistic of individuals

202

no less than of the rest of us. "Go away," says the ego to itself. "But," it continues still speaking to itself, "how can I get away from you, when I am you?" "But get away," comes the irritated reply. To which the ego, still in rancorous conversation with itself, retorts, "Even if I could, you would do yourself wrong, for you would miss me just as much as you find me in the way." The ego continues, "You must stand in the relation of 'thou' to me." But it adds, "When you stand in that relation, you are a hateful figure, no 'thou' at all, but an obstructive 'it'." How can one win in such a game? And what has domination to do with it? The narcissist covers up the struggle. But anyone who has learned something from Freud knows that the strategy does not work, for the struggle moves easily from the sphere of the subjective to the objective, and it turns out soon enough that it is others who are needed and yet stand in the way.

It should be obvious from the preceding considerations that the failure to reckon with the hidden nature of our drives impairs Marcuse's notions of reason and the good society at their roots. The reason that a reasonable man needs to control his life must be a generous reason, free from bigotry and arrogance, instinct with a sense of its fallibility, aware that loyalty to reason is all too often beyond ordinary men and frequently, when the demand is for absolute loyalty, a most unreasonable demand. The reason a man needs must also be aware that it must be sympathetic to the difficulties men meet in their worldly journey, must also be to some extent tolerant of their waywardness, must be charitable to their neuroses, understanding of their cosmic tantrums and their social gripes. Above all, the reason a man wants must be a reason that understands how ready a man is to destroy himself and how prompt he is to read into his fellows his own weaknesses and vices, how ready a man is to cover up his deficiencies by making demands of others that he himself could not possibly meet.

The failure to reckon with the hidden nature of our drives affects Marcuse's conception of the good society, because he does not take into consideration, in his dream of the millennium, that socially speaking men find it much less easy to get along with one another than is desirable for peace or at least

203

for a temporary truce. Schopenhauer said that human beings are gregarious porcupines. He should have said that we are not only gregarious but bristling porcupines. We need to get near one another but when we do we manage inevitably to hurt one another. Were we to accept Marcuse's program, we would still have to face what we face daily now: the tensions, petty hatreds, jealousies, envies, malices, ill-wills which are part of the texture of social life, and so far as one man has been able to discover, an ineffaceable, an indefeasible, an infrangible, an ineradicable, an irrefragable, an uneraseable part of social intercourse.

THIS ESSAY WAS UNDERGOING ITS FINAL REVISIONS WHEN *An Essay on Liberation* was published, a book to which I believe it is worth devoting a few pages. In the Preface Marcuse tells us that he has attempted

> to develop some ideas first submitted in *Eros and Civilization* and in *One-Dimensional Man,* then further discussed in "Repressive Tolerance" and in lectures delivered in recent years, mostly to student audiences in the United States and in Europe.

The first remark about this book is that it does not contain any development whatever of ideas submitted earlier, either in the two books or in the essay mentioned. What we find that is new is the worthless effort to trace morality to a posited biological source already considered and a few, purely surface, innovations that throw some light on Marcuse's recent career. The first of these, because closer to the surface than the others, is the tone of the book. The "Great Refusal" is still one of the dramatis personae in the continuing arraignment of our society, but it is no longer the personification of ineluctable defeat. One is able to notice now, by contrast, in retrospect, that between 1964, at least, and the publication of this book, his work has been mouldy with self-pity. This must be the reason that the gloom in this book is thinner although not yet gone altogether. The recent events have given Marcuse a hope that only the future can show to be true or false. The student riots —and no doubt the role that his thought has played in them— make him hope that there is still a chance of bringing down the edifice of our civilization. He is aware of the fact that the wrecking of our world is not going to be easy. But he no longer thinks it is impossible. While the sun of a new day has not yet begun to shine, for there are no streams of human blood flowing in the gutter as yet, no heaps of repressively tolerated cadavers waiting for the bulldozer to dig the mass grave, there are faint glimmers discernible. The night is breaking. Our monstrous society may yet be brought down. I leave it to the psychoanalysts among my readers to connect the somewhat brighter mood of the Great Refuser with his inclusion along with the other two M's, Marx and Mao, in the intellectual triumvirate leading the legions of destruction.

Another feature is as unexpected as it is welcome. Some of his friends must have been working hard helping revise the impenetrable prose of our nihilist. In this new book there are still some passages through which the reader must cut trail. But the undergrowth is not as thick, and past the impenetrable patches the exhausted reader can, before reaching a clearance, discern light ahead. There is, however, one feature of this book with which "the kids"—as I believe they call themselves—will not be very happy. In *One-Dimensional Man* Marcuse used foreign quotations in the text, chiefly French, but he gave translations in footnotes at the bottom of the page. In this book he makes no concession to the bilingual condition of "the kids" who know only two languages, American English and the language of four-letter words.

Another difference is that the book is couched in a new rhetoric, that should be less ridiculous to some of his readers and less offensive to others. The promises he made in *Eros and Civilization,* should we achieve liberation, are no longer made in the old, pseudo-scientific language. They are still made and they add up to the same old song and dance. But the old lingo has been replaced by a more decorous, and if taken in the traditional sense and not in his own, by a speciously more acceptable formulation. In place of the frankly erotic soteriology about polymorphous and narcissistic reëroticizing which was misleading to the innocent, Marcuse has put "a new sensibility," which he calls "aesthetic," in both senses of the term, that of "pertaining to the senses," and that of "pertaining to art." This is an improvement. If what he wanted was to convert people to his ideology, it was wrong to start by shocking the squares and by arousing the sense of the ridiculous in the reader who knew what the terminology meant. The new terminology gives the meaning clearly enough and with less danger of misinterpretation from the kids who are not at all eager to free themselves "from the tyranny of the genital," and who therefore are apt to interpret narrowly his physiological terms. He still believes that the good life is the life of pleasure, the life of sensual gratification. But the term "aesthetic," in its etymological meaning, leads the mind from sexually rooted sensuality to generalized sensuality, which is what he always meant. The change is, in substance, of no moral significance for, as noted earlier, a life dedicated to the pursuit of sensual gratification can only commend itself to a man who has lost all faith in the dignity of man and can find no other difference between man and his fellow animals than that of quantitative superiority in skill, and the ability, which other animals lack, of providing a rationalization for their way of life. The improvement in language makes the thesis easier to read but not to take.

22

How can one account for the anomaly that is embodied in a man like Marcuse? Nothing short of the complete psychoanalytic dossier could give us an adequate idea of the reason for the man's vitriolic hatred of our world. It is desirable, however, to speculate, because Marcuse, endowed with a superior (if not fine) mind and broad learning, is an excellent representative of a type: the contemporary nihilist. A less able person would not serve the purpose; he could be dismissed because of his mediocrity. I think of these people as the termites of our world, eating away at the uprights of our social edifice, weakening it, until it will come down and crush us all, including some of them. It should be of immense value for us who are concerned with the preservation of what remains of the institutions of our civilization, to discover, if we can, the forces that shape the type.

The following suggestion may help explain Marcuse's corrosive nihilism. It is hardly necessary to point out that the suggestion is speculative and to prove or disprove it evidence that I do not claim to possess would be required. The suggestion is simply that Herbert Marcuse's bitterness comes from the world's failure to recognize him as God. I am quite serious about this hunch.

But how does this account for Marcuse and his followers? It does in this way: Their projection of what ought to be is the result, not of a hard-headed, objective examination of reality and its probabilities, but of a proud, non-comparative demand made of it to satisfy unyielding desires. This is what the world owes me—the world owes it, and it owes it to me; and I am not going to settle for anything less. If you ask one of these absolutists why they think the world owes them anything, when they have exiled themselves voluntarily, they have no answer. But you suspect that the answer is to be found in the unqualified environmentalism that they took in with their mothers' milk. Since reality, present or future, is not likely to live up to a millenarian vision, it is rejected as totally evil. That what Marcuse and his followers expect of a future reality has nothing to do with what has been or is, but only with their ideas *in vacuo,* with overweening demands of society and individuals, with the borborygmus of their intellectual dyspepsia. But these considerations do not trouble them at all. They have the right to demand the ideal, and they are not going to be put off with anything less than what they want.

An adequate understanding of Marcuse's total rejection of everything that is must include the realization that it is a condition of adolescence which the negative thinker never outgrows. The rejection flows from the fact that reality refuses to live up to a deductive pattern of illusions and delusions drawn from books and compacted into a condemnation of a world that does not yield to them. Which is not, of course, to approve of the mind that accepts everything that *is* simply because *it* is.

Let us take, in the random fashion in which they come to my mind, only a few of the generous causes that our society espouses earnestly and to which our ancestors were indifferent. The reason for this exercise is obvious; it plots the direction of our improvements. But before enumerating them, it is necessary to bear in mind, if we are to be fair to the past, that the fact that we are interested in causes they were not interested in does not necessarily mean, by itself, that we have grown in the depth and breadth of our sympathy and pity for our fellow beings. Our ancestors probably were as much concerned with their fellow beings as we are, but they believed that attention should be paid to what was most important and for them it was the health of the soul. Discount for hypocrisy and greed disguised as spiritual charity (the Inquisition confiscated the wealth of its victims) and all the other faults that men are heir to, in the past men were no doubt as honest in their beliefs as we are in ours. The greater secular concern we show, therefore, does not by itself give us the right to judge our ancestors as cruel. For all our secular philanthrophy, the record of the last three-quarters of a century is no basis for comparative self-gratulation.

The most obvious of our concerns with our fellow beings is our attitude towards slavery and the civil rights movement of our century, which is a continuation of the process that began in the Nineteenth Century with the anti-slavery movement. This movement is one that has exerted its force in the advanced society that Marcuse hates. Another expression of the same movement is our attitude towards colonialism, an attitude that can be credited not merely to weakness or self-interest, but in part at least to a genuine growth of decency towards our fellow beings. A good many Americans are sincerely anti-colonialists, some indeed are fanatical and stupid in their attitudes. But I cannot conceive of an American of average decency who would today approve the Belgium of Leopold. There is an interpretation advanced by the New Left to the effect that foreign aid and the work of the Peace Corps are the new forms of imperialism. To say that the interpretation is wacky is to let it off too easily. Or take our concern for the aged, and the physically and the mentally ill. Or take the revolt we have seen occurring during our own lifetime against what we now take to be hobbling moral codes. Or take our concern for the conditions of life in the ghettos. Granted that not enough may have been accomplished as yet, is it not a serious beginning in the right direction? We have started to think honestly and hard about the solution to this problem. Or take the effort that is being made, at the very moment I write, for broadening the educational opportunities of the mass of the underprivileged population. The haste and sentimentalism with which the bleeding-hearts have thrown themselves into the correction of this iniquity is going to cost a heavy price in the very near future—a price we have hardly begun to pay in the threat of destruction of our universities. But the desirability of broadening the opportunities cannot be denied because of the lack of wisdom with which the effort has been carried out. Or take last, but by no means least, the enormous advances we have made in physics and biology and in the rest of the genuine sciences, and in medicine. We may be in for a reaction against science, but its triumphs cannot be denied for that reason. Or the advances in technology, to meet urgent, practical needs. The Luddite attitude that seems to be spreading is no valid ground for denying the positive value of technology. Practical needs could never be met satisfactorily by a people whose imagination is shackled to the crassly utilitarian urges of the "realist" who sees reality steadily and sees it meanly.

The total negation involves a conspiratorial theory of society. The Affluent Society has been created by men who will not let go their power, and since they cannot keep up scarcity they will use the immense productivity contemporary machines give us to forge different chains, but chains no less effective than those that engineering broke. But the conspiratorial theory is no more sound than the devil theory of history. It has great advantages, since it enables those that espouse it to do a lot of explaining with simple laws and easily handled masses of pseudo-facts; it enables them also to whip themselves into the fury, outrage and self-righteousness they seemingly so much enjoy. It arranges the facts, true and imagined, into two columns, the evil ones and the good ones. But as an explanatory theory capable of giving us knowledge it has very little value. And even as a descriptive theory, its value is low. Since it chooses the facts it recognizes and exaggerates them out of all

211

semblance to reality, the conspiratorial theory of society reeks of paranoia. The mind that produced that theory may be sane. The theory is not.

This is not to say, let me repeat, since this is the kind of thought that is easily attributed by the negative thinkers to those who point to the achievements of our civilization, that ours is a perfect society. It is not, and what is more, probably it never will be. For the products of the human mind and artifice can never be perfect, never. We have evil enough and to spare. But evil does not constitute the warp and woof of our social fabric. The paranoid picture painted by the prophet of the New Nihilism is not true of it. And again notice carefully that I am speaking of the picture as paranoid. Whether the prophet is or is not I do not know and I am not interested in asserting.

We know that manufacturers get together to raise prices and that campaigns are planned with great skill on Madison Avenue to launch a new product on a national scale—a new detergent or candy bar or toothpaste. Union leaders, for all their pious drivel, are motivated by personal selfish motives as well as by the desire to improve the condition of their men. And we know that clergymen come together annually to discuss their interests, as do the Mafiosi, the heads of police departments, state governors and teachers of philosophy. But the rulers of our world, the *de jure* and the *de facto* rulers, are too busy running their instruments, their corporations, political parties, the executive and the judiciary, they are too busy staying on top and not presenting too large a target to their opponents, to have time for midnight cabals in dim basements in which the shape and weight and the mode of fastening the shackles they intend to clamp on their victims are discussed.

To assume that our world is the product of a monstrous conspiracy is to give those who are said to conspire greater intelligence, broader vision, more malignant intentions, more power, than they could possibly possess. Bankers, the heads of great corporations, politicians, all the way from men of national stature down to the most mephitic ward-heeler, no doubt possess an above-average amount of ambition, managing ability, and a

212

degree of determination. But they are human beings, not devils.

Who would want to deny that there is iniquity in our world? Of course there is, as there has always been among men, and short of a miracle there always will be among all peoples. There are men and individuals and families that succeed in placing themselves above the law. A young man can let his companion drown under the most puzzling circumstances and he can get off with a two-months suspended sentence. Some of his constituents cry because he is the object of well-merited criticism. I actually heard a woman crying on the squawk box because anyone dared suggest that the man is not fit for public office. The politicians get into the swing. A man flies from Paris to help him write a phony speech that evades the issue. He is too valuable a piece of property—as they say in show biz—to let such a trivial thing as the death of a young woman turn him into spoiled goods.

On the other hand, a President can be booed off a second term, a Supreme Court Justice can be made to resign without impeachment, and Senators are sent to jail. We do not live in Heaven, nor ever will. But we live in a relatively good world, equipped with self-corrective devices. These work no better than other human devices, which is to say that they are not perfect either. But we live in a world far different from the hell Marcuse and his shills say it is. American citizens are human, with human faults and virtues. They are human in their selfishness, in their greed, in the limitations of their moral imagination, and even in the power they wield. For a brief decade the United States was the most powerful nation that history has a record of. But it refused the responsibilities of power. This refusal is nothing to be proud of, but it indicates that in the Darwinian world of international politics in which men have lived as long as there have been nations, Americans tied their hands voluntarily, and suffered betrayal at home and abroad, without falling back on the brutality that other people would have resorted to, could they have commanded the power the Americans had. Americans are humans in their defects and vices, as well as in their virtues and their virtue—their *virtú*.

23

I LEFT FOR ONE OF THE LAST CHAPTERS OF THIS ESSAY TWO general considerations that are of the utmost importance for a correct evaluation of Marcuse's negative thought: the nature of his "style" and the quality of the mind displayed in his pages. Those acquainted with his work need no reminder that the word "style" applied to Marcuse's prose is not employed eulogistically, for he writes merciless jargon. If a unique idiosyncratic manner of expression constitutes "style," Marcuse has style, for his prose is inimitable. In Chapter 2 of *Fads and Foibles in Modern Sociology,* entitled "Verbal Defects: Obtuse Jargon and Sham Scientific Slang," Pitirim Sorokin did not give us an example of Marcuse's thought. But what Sorokin has to say about modern sociology applies, without any need for alteration, to Marcuse's prose.

Seldom easy to understand, when intelligible Marcuse's

prose has the grace of a pregnant hippopotamus trying to dance "The Death of a Swan." One often has to read a sentence, a paragraph, a page, several times to make sure that he has understood it. And on more than one occasion, one reader at least gave up, having to content himself with a very vague idea of the meaning concealed behind the thick, impenetrable verbal undergrowth. Words like "facticity," and "liberalist," are used frequently by a man with a tin ear for language. Substitute "liberal" for "liberalist" and the meaning seems to be the same; use a round-about substitute for "facticity," and the prose becomes lighter. The word "social" is sometimes used by Marcuse; but more often than not the word employed is "societal," thus giving the sentence in which it is employed unnecessary weight. Marcuse criticizes the reifications found in the work of men with whom he disagrees; but his own thought consists of a systematic reification of forces, processes, events and institutions, which he compacts into solid things. These things turn out to be either all good or all bad. Seldom are they what one knows them to be, a mixture of both. If *la vérité reste dans le nuances,* there is very little *vérité* in his pages. When the jargon is rendered out, what is left in lean English frequently turns out to be easy, if not obvious.

The quality of Marcuse's style is no discovery of mine. The ambivalent admirer to whom I referred above, Robert W. Marks, writes that: "Many of his sentences can be deciphered only after long study; and their content, when finally disclosed, turns out to be either debatable or trivial." (*The Meaning of Marcuse,* p. 4) And a reviewer in the *Times Literary Supplement* of London put it in a typically dry English way when he wrote:

> Some students will find Professor Marcuse's writing rather heavy going; seminal ideas are advanced in an elusive and vague form and in jargon of which this is a sample: "Mechanization and rationalization of labour could free an ever greater quantum of individual energy (and time) from the material work process and allow an expenditure of this energy and time for the free play of human faculties beyond the realm of material production."

215

"This could mean," writes the anonymous reviewer, "that with the progress of technology the worker will enjoy more leisure." I do not know whether the reviewer intended these lines to be also an example of a seminal idea. I doubt it.

For the sake of the stylistic exercise, let us take a detailed look at the strengths and graces of the Marcusean prose. Its weight is obtained by the use of such leaden and long terms —in Marcusean language, such ponderous and polysyllabic language—as we find in the following sentence: "The most conspicuous social mobilization of aggressiveness, the militarization of the affluent society," or the phrase, "This is no longer the classical heroizing of killing . . ." The word "heroizing" is a relatively small word, not to be compared in length with "militarization," or "mobilization," but for its size, it can do as well as big fat verbal slobs like "militarization." However, Marcuse has considerably bigger hardware in his armory. One rule of Marcuse's "style" seems to be: "Never use five or six words where fifteen or twenty can be used; never use a light word or a short one where a heavy one or a long one can be used. Monosyllables, unless they are prepositions or articles, must be avoided at all cost, and no effort is to be spared to drag in a big word if it can be fitted. If you want to be a deep thinker, that's the way to do it." Thus Marcuse achieves what we may refer to in Marcuse's patois as the ponderification of the out-put of his mental gyrations through the polysyllabification of jargonical terminology. I am of course aware that any attempt to emulate Marcuse is hopeless. One can use big words, but Marcuse's cacophony cannot be matched. Neither can the impenetrability of his idiolect.

Immediately below I transcribe two relatively short passages of pure Marcusean prose. Although two passages cannot give the reader a fair idea of the unnecessary verbal density, the gratuitously impenetrable verbiage, in which Marcuse expresses himself, and much less can they give him an idea of the extraordinary effort required to keep in one's mind with some clarity what he is trying to read, the passages will give him something of a sample of the kind of undergrowth through which he has to cut trail if he is going to understand our author. But please bear in mind, dear reader, as you go through these passages, that this kind of writing goes on page after page, essay after essay, or chapter after chapter, mercilessly, relentlessly, pitilessly.

Marcuse is discussing freedom and obligation. And he regales us with the following flood of sweet enlightenment:

> Real freedom for individual existence (and not merely in the liberalist sense) is possible only in a specifically structured polis, a "rationally" organized society. In consciously politicizing the concept of existence, and deprivatizing and deinternalizing (*Ent-Innerlichung*) the liberalist, idealist conception of man, the totalitarian view of the state represents progress—progress that leads beyond the basis of the totalitarian state, propelling the theory beyond the social order that it affirms. As long as it remains within the latter's bounds, the progress operates regressively; the process of politicizing and deprivatizing annihilates individual existence instead of truly raising it to "universality." This becomes clear in the antiliberalist concept of freedom. (*N*, p. 39)

All I can say is that I hope so: I mean, I hope it becomes clear. It is lucky I am not asked to give either a "liberalist" or an "antiliberalist" translation of this pellucid passage, for the effort would surely end in deprivatizing and internalizing me, and may even annihilate my individual existence. I have been trying to learn Marcusean patois for some time. The effort has not been too successful. It must be that I have no gift for languages—at least for languages outside the Indo-European family.

Here is a second jewel:

> The philosophy of the bourgeois era was founded by Descartes as a subjective and idealist one, and this resulted from an inner necessity. Every attempt to ground philosophy in objectivity, in the sphere of material reality, without attacking the real presuppositions of its conceptual character, i.e. without integrating into the theory a practice aimed at transformation, necessarily surrenders its rationally critical character and becomes heteronomous. This fate befell the material doctrine of essence; it led, just as with positivism, to the subjection of theory to the

217

"given" powers and hierarchies. With regard to knowledge, the basic meaning of the intuition of essence is that it "lets itself be given" its object, that it passively accepts it and binds itself to it as "something absolutely given." That which gives itself in evident "congruent unity" (*Deckungseinheit*) is "at the same time absolute Being, and the object that is now the object of such Being, such pure essence, is to an ideal degree adequately given." The intuition of essence is (despite the "freedom" of ideational variations) receptive. At the apex of philosophy, the receptivity of the intuition of essence replaces the spontaneity of the comprehending understanding that is inseparable from the idea of critical reason. (Ibid., p. 62)

It's high time, I would say, that the spontaneity of the comprehending understanding be replaced by something, for it has totally failed to comprehend or to understand. But it is very doubtful whether the receptivity of the intuition of essence will do much better. Anyhow, if the reader feels as I do, desperate, he gave up some time ago the hope of getting to the apex of philosophy. He is quite ready to try anything, anything whatever, to get out of the flood of verbiage that threatens to carry him, drowning, to the abysmal bottom of pure nescience.

When one tries to stand back and look at the substance of Marcuse's thought, he discovers that, as social critic, the man is endowed with a very coarse mind—or to be more precise, the reader discovers that beginning with *One-Dimensional Man*, and in all that he has written since, Marcuse's pages display the working of a very coarse mind. But let me warn the reader that it is not easy to distinguish the impenetrable verbiage from the coarseness of his thought. They are not, as Marcuse would put it, "two dimensions" of the same mind. Decidedly not. They are Siamese twins: wherever one goes the other goes.

But I'd better explain further, for the judgment I am making is based on distinctions not always recognized. Recently the editor of a social research review requested a contribution from me, and upon reading the essay objected to my referring in the space of a few lines to Marcuse's erudition and the coarseness of his mind. It was a contradiction, he wrote me. But

218

of course there need be no contradiction if we bear in mind that voluminous learning may go with a mind capable or incapable of making discriminations. Further, the capacity to make discriminations may be exercised in one field of inquiry and not at all in another. Again, an analphabet may have a very fine mind, for book knowledge does not necessarily instill finesse of response. If we human beings were all of one piece, if passions did not rend us, if hatred and love did not direct our capacity to perceive, the distinctions we would have need of to classify the kinds of minds there are would be few. But no classification anterior to the analysis of the quality of a given mind can do justice to its specific nature. One sometimes hears that love is able to discern virtues in its object that indifference overlooks. But hatred also can see, where indifference or love can be blind. If I want a very thorough account of a man's character, I would deprive myself of it if I refused to hear his enemies.

Thus, Pascal's distinction between the heart and the reason is only the beginning of a long story that I cannot stop here to tell in full. Let it suffice to say that such facile couplings as learning and finesse of mind are the products of minds that are themselves somewhat coarse. If a fine mind is aware of distinctions in a given area of discourse, the coarse mind is not; it thinks in terms of unqualified assertions, of apodictic convictions, in terms of very black blacks and blinding whites. But let me iterate that a mind may be coarse in one area of thought and very fine in another. Thus, one of the finest and most creative minds of our century was the mind of Sigmund Freud. The story of the development of his thought is the story of the deepening and correcting of his ideas, the qualifying of them, the noting of complexities overlooked when a problem was first broached. But when Freud turned to religion, his thought was as coarse as that of the village atheist. His intense animus prevented him from seeing why some of the finest and most powerful minds of Western civilization have been deeply religious. On the subject of morality Freud cannot be taken seriously. He failed to notice the important difference between moral conformity—the introjection of regnant values—and the reflection on issues for which no rules can be found or, when they are found, they are judged to be inappropriate. This failure indicates that Freud had no adequate knowledge of moral phenomena. But one admirer of his at least does not hold that on the subject of morality Freud gave evidence of coarseness of thought. He merely gave evidence of paucity of knowledge. On the subject of religion, on the other hand, Freud's thinking was inadmissible because it was coarse. Lacking humility towards the subject, he was blind to the objective factors in response to which the religious man conceives of the idea of God. And I mention Freud, let me repeat, to suggest that a mind that is enormously creative and quiveringly sensitive about some subjects can be unspeakably coarse about others.

In *Reason and Revolution* Marcuse displayed wide knowledge of his subject and a scholarly mind. The coarseness of his work begins with *One-Dimensional Man,* although it can be found in passages written previously. And the coarseness is not difficult to trace to its source. It is no doubt to be found in his hatred of the world in which he was forced to live. Hatred, no doubt, makes him sensitive to iniquities of our world that we may not be sufficiently sensitive to. And if the purpose of this essay were to analyze the quality of the world we live in, it would be necessary to give his indictment careful attention, for none of his charges can be dismissed as utterly without some substance.

In the passage I am about to transcribe, it is not easy to see whether the charge he makes against our world arises from his lack of discernment of the situation he attacks or from the language in which the charge is made. Marcuse tells us that one of the signs of evil of our society is "the brutalization of language" that it has perpetrated. That a phrase like "the brutalization of language" makes its contribution to the brutality of the language he is excoriating, apparently escapes him. But let me quote the paragraph in which he speaks of the brutalization of language, from which I have gathered already the lovely blossoms I exhibited above. It is average Marcusean prose, not picked for its superior impenetrability or for the harshness of its long, abstract terms. It is cacophonous, but cacophony is a quality that is never absent from his writing. It is found here, but not to an exceptional degree.

220

I mentioned, as the most conspicuous social mobilization of aggressiveness, the militarization of the affluent society. This mobilization goes far beyond the actual draft of manpower and the buildup of the armament industry; its truly totalitarian aspects show forth in the daily mass media which feed "public opinion." The brutalization of language and image, the presentation of killing, burning, and poisoning and torture inflicted upon the victims of neocolonial slaughter is made in a common-sensible, factual, sometimes humorous style which integrates these horrors with the pranks of juvenile delinquents, football contests, accidents, stock market reports, and the weatherman. This is no longer the "classical" heroizing of killing in the national interest, but rather its reduction to the level of natural events and contingencies of daily life. (*N*, p. 259)

The passage needs no translation. Its meaning is clear. Marcuse's criticism deserves little attention since it fails to take into account the layout of a paper, the various needs it meets, the diversity of readers who buy it. But let that go. What is interesting is that Marcuse can discern the brutality of language that is displayed anywhere but in his own prose.

One more example of coarse thinking. This time the coarseness is expressed through vague and preposterous charges that "vitiate," as he would put it, the indictment because they are such unqualified interpretations of history. Marcuse wrote in all seriousness a phrase that I have already used in this essay. I shall quote the whole paragraph from which this phrase comes. It is worth pondering. He has told us that it is within a social situation that forces develop that achieve change. And his general thesis is that in our society the movement towards change has been "contained" in a diabolic manner: by granting the members of the society what they want.

Now it is precisely this new consciousness, this "space within," the space for the transcending historical practice, which is being barred by a society in which subjects as well as objects constitute instrumentalities in a whole that has its *raison d'être* in the accomplishments of its overpowering productivity. Its supreme promise is an ever-more-comfortable life for an ever-

221

growing number of people who, in a strict sense, cannot imagine a qualitatively different universe of discourse and action, for the capacity to contain and manipulate subversive imagination and effort is an integral part of the given society. Those whose life is the hell of the Affluent Society are kept in line by a brutality which revives medieval and early modern practices. For the other, less underprivileged people, society takes care of the need for liberation by satisfying the needs which make servitude palatable and perhaps even unnoticeable, and it accomplishes this fact in the process of production itself. Under its impact, the laboring classes in the advanced areas of industrial civilization are undergoing a decisive transformation, which has become the subject of a vast sociological research. (*O-D M*, p. 23)

What is unpardonable about our society is that a great majority of its members are happy because they get what they want, and want more of what they have. This is criminal, and the crime, as Marcuse would say, has several "dimensions." First, blue- and white-collar workers have been given things without Marcuse having first been consulted. Unpardonable, of course. Second, the productivity of our society has negated, as Marcuse would say, class conflict, thus vitiating—I am afraid Marcusean language is contagious—Marx and Marcuse at the practical level. And I say, it has vitiated Marx and Marcuse's views "at the practical level" because it is self-evident that neither Marx nor Marcuse can be theoretically vitiated, since what they hold is truth. But what is wrong with giving workers —blue- and white-collar—what they want? I have already given a hint of the answer above: What is wrong is that they are happy in a world that Marcuse has decreed is not a world in which a Marcusean can be happy.

I quoted the passage about the revival of brutality of late medieval and early modern times, not because it puts Marcuse's thesis with unusual lucidity—which it does—but because it is an excellent example of Marcuse's punctilious historical scholarship. We are kept in line by brutality. And if you have not been put to the question as an inquisitor would have done, you happen to be one of the lucky ones that J. Edgar or the bravos of the CIA overlooked. Lucky you. The rest of us have had our sessions with the iron maiden, the wheel, the thumbscrews, our feet in the flames, and a number of other refinements employed by "the Military-Industrial Complex" to see to it that we behave and quit bitching because we only have two cars and want a third. While threatening us with devices that revive medieval and early modern practices, the hell of the Affluent Society gives us what we want. And let's ask again, what is it that we want? Why, two cars with ferocious names and the iron maiden, a split-level house and the wheel, another TV set and the thumbscrews. I confess I am a little confused. But one thing I am clear about: You and I and the rest of us are kept in line with devices revived from late medieval and early modern times. It should not happen to a man who lives in the Affluent Society. But it does. Marcuse says it does.

The passage is wonderful. I would call it "insightful," if the term were one I allowed myself to use. It is wonderful because of its historical accuracy. It is known that J. Edgar has studied *au fond* the techniques of the Spanish Inquisition and has learned Chinese to study Chinese techniques of putting a man to the question. It is also wonderful because the passage is so accurate about the victims of the Affluent Society. We all are kept in line. Not you and I, and your family and mine, but every Tom, Dick and Herb that lives in our world, every one. Further, the statement about our society is a comparative historical statement—contrary to what I claimed above to the effect that Marcuse makes no comparative judgments. Marcuse says that our society has revived practices of the past and names the period, late medieval and early modern. Could a historical statement be more precise than that? To ask for more is to ask Marcuse to crawl through the swamp of historical facts.

The passage is wonderful, let there be no doubt about it. But it is also an excellent illustration of a coarse piece of thinking.

How anyone can take seriously Marcuse's accusations against our society without introducing radical qualifications strains the understanding until one remembers, not what he says, but "the kids" and the lumpen-intelligentsia of the academy that read him. Take "the kids" first. Facing the prospect of having to come to grips with an alien world, secure in the knowledge that they, with their one-and-a-half to two-and-a-half decades of experience behind them, could have done much better than their elders and the generations that preceded them did, brought up in abundance without serious responsibilities, and taught that there are no objective maxims by which conduct can be guided, Marcuse's authoritarian condemnation of the world gives the kids comfort. Whether they have the fortitude to unravel the thought of the master is doubtful. But they do get its general trend and numerous slogans. The trend they agree with, the slogans they use. They know more or less clearly that he encourages their gripes and protects their dreams. He sanctions their refusal to consider with humility the dubieties, confusions, conflicting values, and contradictions of aims of an imperfect and disordered world, full of threats and traps. These faults are unnecessary. All faults are unnecessary. "Reason" can do away with them. He makes everything black and white for them, and that is how they like it: friends all on one side, enemies all on the other. That can be handled mindlessly, in full rage. And what he can't handle with his simplifications or what he ignores, they can ignore. He suggests that they represent the hope of the world and in their ignorance, their untested arrogance, and in their gullibility, they believe him.

How many of these wreckers there are in the United States today is not known, since the class is not a well defined one, and it becomes larger or smaller with varying circumstances. But at the core there is a group dedicated to destruction. And there is reason to fear that they will sooner or later accomplish what they have in mind: destroy the universities. The destruction of the universities is the first step towards the destruction of our world since these institutions are the heart of our civilization, which could not continue for long without the training they give the citizen in all the fields in which they are active in research and teaching.

I have not read anything that is enlightening about the motivation of these wreckers, and do not expect to, chiefly, perhaps, because those who are interested in the alarming phenomenon are not altogether out of sympathy with the wreckers. Could you expect the administration of Bryn Mawr, for instance, or a majority of its teaching staff, to give us an analysis of the psycho-sociological forces that make a nihilist? Bryn Mawr used to be a distinguished institution. But it was not satisfied with its educational distinction. It decided to tell the nation on which side of the present conflict it was. And its announcement could not have been more eloquent. It appointed as the Head of its African Studies Program a man well

225

known as a communist. No one properly qualified has claimed for this man, Herbert Aptheker, that he is a scholar. His record indicates that he is a theoretician of revolution. If Bryn Mawr were the only instance of this kind of will to self-destruction, the matter would be serious enough. But the fact is that in probably all the universities of America there are to be found fifth columns of men actively dedicated to destruction. These men are energetic and so far they have been fairly successful in accomplishing what they have set out to do. Their success is in part to be traced to the fact that they are surrounded by an apparently apathetic majority whose tepid surface indifference to the wrecking minority barely conceals its sympathy with the wreckers.

Surrounded by such men the fifth columnists are sufficiently influential to block measures to suppress effectively the chaos the rioters create. This allows the rioters to function in a favorable medium. When anyone tries to direct attention to this fact, the professors go immediately on the defensive, by opposing in the name of *ad hoc* "wisdom" and "reason" and unprincipled prudence, efforts to deal effectively with the nihilistic outrages and destructiveness of the wreckers. Propose severe disciplinary action in a faculty meeting. No, for the sake of your safety, do not propose it in a faculty meeting; you would be in for a very rough time. Try it with the next professor you meet in the hall, a quiet and reasonable man, a liberal like the whole lot of them, but a nice enough guy whom you occasionally talk to without displeasure. The professor breaks out into a wild verbal freshet or, more exactly, a river at the height of its spring flood, carrying heavy logs of "buts," "ifs," "on the other hands" and the numerous other floating dangers that threaten to knock you down and drown you. When he has exhausted himself apologizing for these malevolent wretches, he is ready with his last apologia: They are trying to tell us something. We ought to listen.

I reply: I know what they are telling us. But there are questions within questions here, and the innermost ones we are not clear about. Nor are they, of course. What they are clearly telling us is that they want to wreck the joint. The alleged

226

causes for the riots—a gymnasium in a park, investment funds, military contracts, employment interviews with graduating seniors—they have told us candidly, and in their standard four-letter-word vocabulary, that they are phony excuses. But why do they want to destroy our world, the world that soon will be theirs? The answer to this question few of us want to hear. And the reason is simple: We do not want to hear that to a large extent it has been the termite work we teachers have been doing for decades and are still doing that is responsible for their conduct. It was we who imparted to them, in the name of enlightenment, the belief that our civilization was worthless. We communicated to them the contempt we had for our values. We never meant that contempt too seriously, but you cannot tell that to an immature mind. He takes you at your word, and your fine "but on the other hands" are disregarded. We showed that contempt in order to assure ourselves that we were superior to the Babbitts around us, that we knew how hollow the values of our ancestors had been, how iniquitous the world they had reared was, and how much better we could do. We tried to do better. And our efforts turned out to be dismal failures. And the failures cannot be hidden from the eyes of the intelligent ones among them.

In the name of freedom from irrational restraints we deprived them of discipline; in the name of generosity we gave them what we should have made them work for if they wanted it; in the name of the truth of the philosophers and the social scientists we taught them that there was nothing objectively valuable and worth maintaining, nothing, and least of all worth maintaining at the greatest risk. A thing was good because one wanted it. This doctrine, interpreted by immature minds, was agreeable truth—there were so many things they wanted that we thought were no good, and so many things they did not want. We communicated to them very clearly that our ancestors had lived for lies, myths, groundless illusions. In an understandable reaction to butchery we revived the old dream of universal peace, but forgot to tell ourselves and them that it takes one to make a fight. We were egalitarians, but could not conceal from ourselves our sense of superiority to those who

227

did not accept our beliefs. We taught them that the world's evil was not in us but in the environment, and here was another truth they really valued, for they inferred from the doctrine what we had been inferring from it all along: that no one was responsible for his actions, that we were all just mixed-up kids because we had been deprived of love or put on the pot too soon, or too late, or not at all, or something equally capable of leading to confusion, alienation and crime, later on; we taught them that all men loved one another because they ought to love one another, and thus we reduced to nothing the contrast between reality and the ideal. But the love of man we taught them was an abstract love, and again they saw through our hypocrisies. They wanted utopia, universal peace, universal brotherhood, and love, because we had taught them that those were the values that decent men espoused, and they saw we were right. But we never hinted to them that men's efforts to realize their dreams had been throughout history a continuously sad story of struggle, frustration, and defeat, no less than of courage, selflessness, and glory. We knew all about words like glory. We had been taught by our critics that the poet who had written that these words embarrassed a man had reached the apex of wisdom. One did not say anything was sacred, one did not believe in glory, and sacrifice was a dirty word since it always was in vain. And this we taught them in the classroom and out of it. It followed in the rioters' minds that if we could not make our noblest dreams come true it was our fault, because we really did not believe in our ideals.

But above all they copped out because they did not want to prepare themselves for the responsibilities and duties and the frustrations that make up adult life. They condemned the liberal orthodoxy, as they had a perfect right to do, because they saw it was a puddle of nonsense, self-deception, self-righteousness, and hope and unrealistic faith. To believe, some teacher of pragmatism had told them, was to act upon our beliefs. While this was true with careful qualifications, they failed to make the qualifications, and simplistically concluded that we could not believe what we said we believed. They believed and they acted. No mere bleeding-hearts, they. From them, action. Columbia, Berkeley, San Francisco State College, Cornell, the University of Illinois at Urbana, the College of the City of New York, Northwestern, and the rest. One loses count.

That the kids should take Marcuse seriously is, then, no mystery. But how can we explain the bedoctored balding heads that take him seriously? How can we account for the professors and administrators who defend his right to shoot his slanderous mouth off in his efforts to destroy our society? How can we explain the blindness of these men to this nihilist's obvious defects? To his exaggerations, his lack of historical perspective, his utter lack of a sense of intellectual fairness, his peevish explosions, his paroxysms of rage at trivialities, the coarseness of his mind, and the fact that he preaches the destruction of our society?

One argument in favor of Marcuse deserves careful notice: the argument from academic freedom. As applied to Marcuse this argument is utterly irrelevant since Marcuse repudiates in advance the code of conduct that allows a man to apply for membership in the academic world. Consider: No science department in the nation would hire a man who announced in advance of his being hired that he did not have the least intention of doing his work with an open mind, who wrote that he did not intend to listen to the criticisms of his hypotheses advanced by his colleagues, because he knew they were wrong and he had contempt for them; and that he had every intention of preventing them from carrying on the experiments they had planned, because he knew in advance of their being performed that they were nonsense. This is an important point: No responsible department of science—and I am speaking about the real sciences, not the psuedo-sciences that are called by their practitioners "the soft sciences"—would hire such a man. Such a man is not a scientist. He is not a scholar. He is unfit for an academic post. But this is what Marcuse the "philosopher" and the "social scientist" declares to be one basic tenet of his thought—tolerance toward the Left, repression of the Right. He knows, and knows in advance, and knows beyond argument, that he is right and those who disagree with him are wrong. Which is to say that he is neither a philosopher nor a

229

social scientist but an intellectual energumen. A man with a closed mind may be fit for any number of things—I do not know whether he is or not, but he may be. But a man with a closed mind is not fit to serve in a philosophy department or in the division of the social sciences of a university. A man like that is not fit to be an academic man. He has already settled the question of freedom by announcing that he does not believe in it. To write that the principle of academic freedom gives a man like Marcuse the right to write and say what he does is a blatant betrayal of academic freedom.

Why then do the academics who defend him go out of their way to protect his right to destroy our world? Either because they do not see what he is trying to do or because they have sympathy with what he is doing. Or because they do not care. Or for a combination of any of these. If there is a fourth alternative, dear reader, you furnish it. I can't think of it.

In any case, the men who defend Marcuse ought to be brought to the bar of judgment. They are irresponsible, if they are not corrupt.

Index

234